Powerful Money Habits

Unleash Financial Freedom

Dr. Stephanie Aldrich

Disclaimer

Although the author and publisher have made every effort to ensure that the information in this book was correct at press time, the author and publisher do not assume and hereby disclaim any liability to any party for any loss, damage, or disruption caused by errors or omissions, whether such errors or omissions result from negligence, accident, or any other cause.

This book is not intended as a substitute for the financial advice of professional financial brokers, planners, and insurance agents.

This book is not intended as a substitute for the medical, marital, or spiritual advice of physicians, psychologists, counselors, therapists, and clergymen. The reader should regularly consult these professionals in matters relating to their physical and mental health, particularly concerning any symptoms that may require diagnosis or medical attention.

978-1-7333770-7-2

Dedication

To those who want financial freedom.

Table of Contents

Introduction

This book is a guide designed to transform your financial life from the ordinary to the extraordinary. Whether you're struggling with debt, stagnant in your savings goals, or simply seeking to enhance your financial stability, this book is your roadmap to financial success. Every chapter will start with a QR code like the one on the next page and will lead you to video training that will help you navigate through the rough financial waters. Don't take these video training sessions or any other page in this book lightly! If you follow what is written in this book, you will find yourself less stressed and more secure about your money habits. It all starts with your mindset, your plan, and your actions towards wealth creation and this book has it all!

In today's world, where financial uncertainty often looms large and economic fluctuations impact everyone, mastering your money is more important than ever. Yet, despite this urgency, many find themselves caught in financial habits that hinder rather than help their aspirations. It's not merely about making more money; it's about making your money work effectively and efficiently for you, an important skill set that most people lack.

"Powerful Money Habits" isn't just another financial advice book that skims the surface of budgeting and saving. Instead, it dives deep into the core practices that can build lasting wealth—habits that have been cultivated by financial experts, successful investors, and ordinary people who have achieved extraordinary financial success.

This book is structured to guide you through the essentials of creating a solid financial foundation, advancing through strategies that leverage your earnings and culminating in sophisticated techniques to safeguard and grow your wealth. Each chapter and corresponding video training session is designed to introduce you to key concepts and practices, followed by actionable steps that you can integrate into your daily life.

From learning to live below your means to investing wisely, from avoiding common financial pitfalls to planning for retirement, "Powerful Money Habits" covers the full spectrum of personal finance. Additionally, this guide provides insights into developing a mindset that embraces abundance, strategic thinking, and proactive financial management.

Prepare to challenge your conventional views on money, overhaul your financial behaviors, and discover habits that are not only powerful but unstoppable in their capacity to transform your financial destiny. Let's embark on this journey together, building one powerful habit at a time, steering you towards a future where financial freedom isn't just a dream—it's your reality. Watch the training below.

If you want to dive even deeper into more training on how to earn more, save more, and build more wealth, I have a FREE masterclass that I did with a group of students that can help you build financial freedom. During this masterclass I'm going to go in depth in the three areas that you need to master to become wealthy. If you miss any one of these three steps, you will fail. It's as simple as that. Watch the training. Absorb the information and then start implementing what is said into your own life. We face a lot of uncertainty in the world right now. People are at each other's throats over political and social issues. Money is tight and the economy is sketchy. But these times aren't any different from previous strife. You too can not only survive but thrive in this environment or any environment if you know what steps to take to build lasting wealth and unforgettable change. Are you ready to take the first step? Go watch the FREE masterclass at PowerfulMoneyHabits.com now. Take your first step now towards financial freedom.

Chapter 1

Common Money Habits

In this opening chapter, we explore the everyday financial behaviors that shape our lives. Most of us engage in a variety of financial habits without much thought—paying bills, shopping for groceries, or even choosing a coffee shop. While these actions might seem trivial on the surface, they are the foundational blocks of our financial health.

Why start with the common? Because understanding and refining these everyday practices is the first step toward transforming your financial landscape. Here, we'll dissect which habits serve us well and which subtly undermine our financial stability. You'll learn how small changes in these daily actions can lead to profound shifts in your financial well-being.

We'll explore habits like budgeting regularly, monitoring spending, saving a portion of every paycheck, and using credit cards wisely—habits you might already know or heard about previously, but perhaps haven't fully mastered or understood their impact. And because of this lack of implementation, you're not financially free yet. This chapter will provide you with a mirror to reflect on your current financial behaviors and the lens to view them critically, identifying areas for improvement.

But this chapter goes beyond merely identifying good and bad habits. It's about understanding the psychology behind our financial decisions, the common pitfalls we encounter, and the societal pressures that shape our spending and saving patterns. By exploring these aspects, you'll gain insights into how you can take control of your finances, making informed and empowered choices. Choices that will lead to wealth creation.

Challenge your assumptions, embrace practical solutions, and start on the path to rewriting your financial story. As we sift through these common money habits, you'll begin to see which behaviors you should continue, which need a tweak, and which should be completely revamped or discarded.

Let's begin this journey by building a strong foundation of healthy, common money habits that pave the way for financial success and a richer life. Watch the training below.

Set Clear Financial Goals

"If you aim at nothing, you'll hit it every time."-Zig Ziglar

Zig is so right. Most of us waste our lives watching TV or scrolling the internet. We also waste our money on things that don't matter because we're bored and want the excitement that comes with buying something new. With the economy uncertain, and inflation out of control, some of us feel like the future is grim and out of our grasp. But what we don't realize is that times are always uncertain, crazy people always vote for other crazy people that have no clue how to run things. It's a fact. But one thing is very clear, we can control our own Universe.

We can control how we spend our money. We can control how much we're saving and how much we're investing. We can control what we buy. Do we wait for a sale? Do we compare prices? Do we even need this item? Do we want to retire in our 40s or 50s? What would that take for us to accomplish that? Do we want to travel? Do we want a beautiful house? Do we want a new car? All these things take money and without a clear plan, none of it will happen. Define what you want to achieve financially in specific, measurable terms and run with it. All these things take money and without a clear plan, none of it will happen. Define what you want to achieve financially in specific, measurable terms and run with it.

Create a Budget

"You can buy anything, but you can't buy everything."-Unknown

I know, budgets suck. It feels like you don't have the freedom to buy what you want. But the questions you must ask yourself are, "Do I ever want to retire? Do I ever want to be financially free and owe no one money? Do I really want to buy this thing that I think will make me happy?"

Once you figure this out, you'll realize that financial freedom comes with a price, and you must pay that price to win. The most important price to pay is to control your money. You only have so much to work with and you must delegate it wisely. America was built on industry and commerce. We thrive in technology and science. But all these things come at a price, and they have cleverly designed marketing messages to keep their hands in your wallet so they can make a profit. I never had a formal written budget until I was 47 years old. And because I finally drank the budget Kool Aid, I was able to pay off my car, my business loans, and my house within 18 months. I would have never accomplished this without a set goal and a written budget. I still budget every month because I have a goal of retiring in 2029 and to do that, I must keep my finances on track. The easiest way to do that is to set a budget and have the discipline to follow it.

Pay Off Debt

***"Debts are like children: the smaller they are the more noise they make."*-Spanish Proverb**

It's so easy to swipe a card and think that you'll pay it off later. It's so easy to sign some papers for a new car or home loan. It's so easy to purchase furniture and pay it off over 18 months. But then the bills come, and you notice that all your money is going out the door to pay bills and loan payments. What happened?

We all want stuff. We all want to feel important. We all want to be pampered. We all want something new. The problem that most of us have is that we want it now. We don't think about how we're going to pay for it because we can borrow money, but that only puts us behind on our wealth-building journey. Marketing campaigns manipulate us into thinking that we aren't enough. That our stuff isn't enough. That others will pity us for not having that new thing. But in reality, we are good enough. Our stuff is good enough. And no one is thinking about you, they're too busy thinking about themselves! Follow Dave Ramsey's baby steps and get yourself out of debt ASAP so you can start living the life you really want and aren't burdened by monthly payments for things you don't even remember buying! Then start saving and pay everything in cash- what a stress relief!

Emergency Fund

"It's nice to have an umbrella on a rainy day."-Stephanie Aldrich

Our emergency fund is like that umbrella on a rainy day. Our kid falls off his bike and breaks his arm. We have a high deductible health insurance plan that only kicks in after that high deductible is paid for. What do we do? No worries, our emergency fund will take care of it. Our furnace goes out and is unrepairable. What do we do? No worries, our emergency fund will buy us a new one. Our business has some cash flow problems and needs a boost. What do we do? No worries, our emergency business fund will help keep us on solid financial ground.

That's what extra money is for. It's to help keep us safe and out of debt when something happens. And something will always happen. It's recommended to have 3-6 months or more saved in both cash and some in a high-yield savings account. This money should never be invested as markets can fluctuate greatly day by day and if we truly need it, we need to know that it's there for us to use. Taking a vacation or buying that new Blackstone griddle is not an emergency. Save that money and then forget about it. It's there as insurance, nothing more. You'll be so glad you have it when you need it!

Live Below Your Means

"There is no dignity quite so impressive, and no independence quite so important, as living within your means."-Sophia Amoruso

The magic sauce of building wealth needs ingredients. One of those ingredients is money to invest. If you live on less than you make, you will have extra money left in your budget to use to invest in your future. It's a very simple concept to understand, but not necessarily an easy concept to carry out in our lives. It takes discipline and courage to say no to things that you may want to buy or want to experience. No, you can't buy that new car because you didn't plan for it yet. No, you can't go out with your friends because you've already spent your 'going out' money this month. No, you can't get your own apartment because it's not in your budget. Saying no to yourself and saying no to other people is not an easy thing to do but is necessary if you want to build wealth. Creating a budget and sticking to it helps you create ways of spending your money differently than if you had no budget. Maybe you don't go out with your friends, but have them over to your place for dinner and drinks afterwards. Maybe you start working a side hustle and save for a newer car or your own apartment. Watching what you spend and making sure you have money to invest every paycheck will guarantee you build wealth.

Insurance

"Term insurance is temporary, but your problem is permanent."-Unknown

Everyone is going to die. Everyone makes mistakes. We have an achy tooth. The storm blew over a tree onto our roof. Someone hit our car in the parking lot. Things happen. It's called life. But life can get in the way of our wealth building and can certainly drain our wallets if we're not prepared. We can spend a little today on insurance or we can spend a lot more if something wrong occurs (and something wrong always occurs.) Make sure you have enough insurance to protect you and your property. This can include medical, car, home, dental, vision, liability umbrella, and even life insurance. I know, it seems like overkill, but you never know when something can happen to you, or your loved ones and you want to make sure you protect your wealth. We live in a very litigious system with 36,000 attorneys graduating from law school every year, amounting to 1.3 million actively practicing attorneys waiting to feed their families by suing you and taking your money. Please don't think that insurance companies are your friends because they're not. They have many ways not to pay you for a claim and you need to make sure that you have documentation including before and after photos as well as receipts to show legitimacy of your claim. Hire an independent agent and have them shop policies for you. Be prepared.

Diversify

"Diversification is protection against ignorance."-Warren Buffett

Diversification means investing in areas that are not correlated to each other so that if one industry or area is affected by the economy, another may not be. This helps to minimize losses as the economic and political forces ebb and flow from day to day. Most people mistakenly think that diversifying their investments means to hold both stocks and bonds, but this isn't what true diversification means. True diversification means that you may own a business. This may mean that you invest in real estate. This may mean you invest in energy syndication. This may mean you invest in precious metals, like physical silver and gold. This may mean you invest in collectibles, like art or cars. Inflation will cause all of these areas to increase in worth, but some will fly over time and make you wealthy, while others will struggle to get off the ground. That's how the world of investing goes. But one thing is certain- it doesn't matter what you invest in, as long as you invest in something. Choose three to five things that are unrelated and guarantee yourself a happy and prosperous future. Make it simple and straightforward, and don't invest in anything you don't understand or could explain to your mom. That will keep you out of trouble and to make sure that your money is working and not lost to stupidity.

Financial Literacy

"You become what you study."
-Robert Kiyosaki

To become wealthy, you must educate yourself. Unfortunately, we're not taught a lot about money in school or college. Even if we study economics or finance, that doesn't mean we know how to build wealth in our personal lives. I had a patient that had graduated with a degree in finance. It was about six months after graduation that I saw him in my office. I asked him what he was doing, and he told me that he was still looking for a job. I asked him, "Didn't school teach you how to make money and get a job?" He said no. He was still at home after he spent thousands and thousands of dollars on an education that failed him.

If you follow the steps I outline in this book, and implement them, there's no way you won't be on your way to a wealthy future. Make sure that you put your money to work and find out the ways to do this. Find people that are building businesses or buying real estate or investing in certain stocks and copy what they're doing. We're lucky that we don't have to reinvent the wheel when it comes to building wealth. Choose a mentor and follow their path to multiply your money. The sooner you get your money working for you, the sooner you won't have to work for your money!

Frugality

"Without frugality none can be rich, and with it very few would be poor." -Samuel Johnson

Frugality doesn't mean being cheap. Frugality doesn't mean drinking water and eating crackers every day to save a buck. Frugality means being intentional with your money and your lifestyle. It means that you spend your money on the things that you love, and you forget about the rest of the stuff that society tells you that you should buy. If you love clothes but don't care about nice cars, you drive a cheaper car and selectively buy nicer clothes. If you love coffee, you spend your money on an expensive espresso machine and forget about going through the drive thru. When you focus your attention on what brings you joy, you realize that there's so many things that you're wasting your money on that don't and you give yourself permission to stop. When you stop, you give yourself the margin that you need to start saving and investing for your future. It's okay to not have the things that other people have. It's okay to not travel and spend on flashy stuff if that doesn't interest you. Spend your money wisely and on the things that make you happy and tirelessly invest the rest so that you can continue enjoying your favorite stuff when you're no longer working. It's that margin that's the magic to financial freedom. Create some today.

Buy Assets

"Don't wait to buy assets. Buy assets and wait."-Ray Brown

Assets put money in your pocket. Liabilities take money out. Throughout this book, I'm going to start opening your eyes to how the wealthy really get wealthy. They think differently than the middle class and it shows in their profit and loss statements. What do they do differently than the middle class? It's simple: they own stuff. I'm not talking about cars, planes, and big houses. I'm talking about owning stuff that makes you rich. Assets that put money in your pocket every month. That's real estate- both commercial and residential. It could be storage units. It could be mobile home parks. It could be hotels and golf courses. It could be farmland and timber. It could be single family homes and it could be large multifamily complexes. They own businesses in different industries. They may make products to sell from manufacturing or they may provide services through franchises. It could be dividend stocks and bonds. It could be in agriculture owning cattle and livestock. It could be in energy where they invest and provide nuclear, solar and wind, or oil to the world. There are so many ways that the rich get richer that it's easy for you and I to get a small slice of the pie for ourselves. Use your money to buy things that pay you, not things that will go in a dump someday. This is the **#1** way to build wealth!

Say No!

"A small leak will sink a great ship."-Benjamin Franklin

Some of us feel obligated to do things. Some of us feel obligated to buy things. If you don't have the time or the money, then why are we feeling obligated? If you're surrounded with social pressure, get rid of it. Pull yourself out of the situation with a simple phrase called NO! It's okay to say no to things that don't serve you, especially if it requires spending money on it. No, we can't afford a travel team. No, we can't afford to go on vacation. No, we can't afford to go to that fancy restaurant tonight. No, we can't afford to buy that expensive coat. No, no, no. When you start living with intentionality, you'll start spending your money differently. If you love Starbucks coffee but don't care about designer purses, then you'll spend your money on Starbucks and not purses if your friend wants a new one. It's all about using money to make you happy, but also using it to build wealth and financial freedom. You can have some things you want, but you can't afford to have everything you want. Don't let frivolous little purchases here and there, sink your wealth creation. Use your mighty dollars to amass a great fortune that will support you for the rest of your life, and not squander it on stuff that will end up in a dump somewhere. Your money is more powerful than that. Harness that power by saying no to stupid crap!

Learn a Second Language

"Two languages open every door along the way."-Frank Smith

People that know multiple languages can interact and engage with international markets and diverse business environments that most people can't associate with due to a language barrier. Many friends that I know learned another language and majored in international business in college and have gone on to high executive careers for large manufacturing companies and have made a lot of money and have traveled around the world. You may be lucky in that your parents speak another language, maybe they immigrated to America from another country. This is an advantage that you must take into consideration as you're choosing your career. Learn this language and use it to build ties with those countries that speak that language. You will be so much more valuable in the marketplace when you can communicate with people from all over the globe. Whether you work for a large corporation or are a private consultant, your language skills are a valuable asset to any business environment. According to Preply.com, multilingual employees earn an average of 19% more than employees who only speak one language. Over time, this could amount to hundreds of thousands, if not millions of dollars more in your retirement accounts over your career.

Call to Action

"Becoming rich is hard. Staying broke is hard. Choose your hard." -Eric Worre

The only way to make money is to earn it. Yes, there's so called "passive income" but to buy the asset that starts giving off cash flow, you must first earn money. This takes action. This takes skill sets that the marketplace wants. This involves solving problems that people have. This takes time, energy and effort. This takes networking. This takes planning. What about wealth accumulation? Again, it takes effort and energy to earn money. It takes discipline to live below your means and invest the rest. It takes planning (through a written budget) to track what money is coming in and what money is going out. It takes education and perseverance to learn how to invest and review how your plan is going. I urge you to not only glance over this book, but start implementing the strategies in it, because I've gone through all of them and have experience in poor money management and through education and experience, have accomplished good money management and wealth accumulation. And you can too! But it's time to take things seriously. It's time to pay attention. It's time to act on the things in this book that you need to accomplish in order to pay off debt and start investing in your future. Do you want to work until you die? Then get busy!

Chapter 2

Not-So-Common Money Habits

We now venture beyond the everyday financial behaviors explored in the first chapter, diving into the less typical practices that can significantly enhance your financial prowess. While the habits discussed previously lay the groundwork, the strategies in this chapter are about building the structure that can elevate your financial life to new heights.

In this chapter, we uncover the habits that aren't on most people's radars—practices that can be game changers. These include automating your investments, leveraging tax-advantaged accounts to the fullest, and mastering the art of credit manipulation. These habits aren't practiced by many, perhaps because they require a bit more knowledge, intention, and discipline. However, the rewards they offer are well worth the effort.

We will explore why these not-so-common habits are rarely adopted and how you can integrate them into your own financial strategy to stand out from the crowd. This chapter is designed to push your financial thinking and planning beyond conventional boundaries. Each habit is dissected to reveal how it contributes to long-term financial security and wealth accumulation. Practical advice and examples from my real life will help you grasp how these practices can be applied in various aspects of your financial life. We'll also touch on the psychological and emotional readiness needed to implement these habits, ensuring you are prepared to embrace and maintain them over the long haul.

Ready to explore the less trodden path of financial excellence? Chapter 2 will equip you with the tools and knowledge to incorporate these powerful, not-so-common money habits into your daily routine, setting the stage for extraordinary financial success. Watch the training below.

Automate

**"Want to simplify your life?
Automate your finances."
-Jackie Kenoyer**

Want to guarantee that you build wealth? Automate your money. Go to your HR department and sign up for direct deposit. Then sign up for auto pay through your bank to pay for your monthly bills. Then set up auto transfers through your bank to save money in your emergency fund and retirement accounts. You can even set up your retirement accounts to automatically buy when there's money transferred in them. Automate, automate, automate. Then you take out your emotions in the process. You know in the back of your mind that there's money working for you and that you are now free to spend what's left over on the things that make you happy. This is why creating a budget is so important to building wealth. Many times, you can set it up once, and then forget about it until it's time for a quarterly review and a yearly net worth calculation. There's no excuse nowadays for building wealth. Automating your finances makes it easy and definite. Stop what you're doing right now, grab all your bills and statements, and get on your computer or phone and set up auto pay accounts right now! Another ingredient to the secret sauce of wealth is using technology like automation to your advantage. Sign up today- you'll be so happy you did!

Review

"Know what you own and why you own it."-Peter Lynch

Building wealth is not a set-it-and-forget-it kind of thing. Yes, I just talked about automating your saving and investing, that's not what I'm trying to say. What I mean is that we all must take a look at our investments and our wealth creation and make sure that we're on track to accomplish our financial goals. This doesn't mean that you're checking your accounts every day as we all know there's daily fluctuations in the economy and markets. What I do is check monthly to make sure I'm saving and investing in a way that builds my wealth. And because I read a lot of financial books and consume a lot of financial videos and podcasts, sometimes my investing areas change a little. Recently I read a book called *The Holy Grail of Investing* by Tony Robbins. If you are an accredited investor making over $200,000 a year in income, I highly suggest reading this book as it opened my eyes to private equity and credit that has exploded my wealth building process.

Review monthly, quarterly, and yearly how your wealth is increasing and make changes where you need to depending on what's happening in your life and your career. Add something or subtract something that will help you stay on your money goals. Track debt elimination and new worth accumulation. It's easy.

Patience

"The most important quality for an investor is temperament and not intellect."-Warren Buffett

The market will crash. Inflation will skyrocket. The housing market will crash. Interest rates will skyrocket. Should you get out of the markets and sit on the sidelines with your money? ABSOLUTELY NOT! Your motto should be that you're in it for the long haul and market and economic fluctuations should bear nothing on your investment strategies. If you really want to build wealth like the pros, you always set aside cash to invest in times when the markets are down, and everything is on sale. When people are afraid, they do stupid things with their money and smart investors take advantage of this and explode their wealth in the meantime. Wealth isn't built overnight. It builds upon itself. So be patient. Be consistent. Take advantage of downturns in whatever market you're investing in. Over time, everything will go up because that's how our capitalistic system works. When the Federal Reserve manipulates the money supply and interest rates, this drives prices up. This causes inflation. That means all prices go up- raw materials, goods you buy at the store, and of course, assets go up. Stocks, real estate, precious metals. Everything goes up. That's a great thing if you're an investor in these things. So when they're down, buy more.

Minimalism

"Love people and use things because the opposite never works."
-The Minimalists

Live simply. Do you need 16 spatulas? Only if you're a professional chef. Do you need 10 black T-shirts? Only if that's your entire wardrobe. Spending your money on duplicates and just-in-case items makes corporations rich and your wallet empty. When you live more simply, you realize that your *stuff* doesn't make you happy. All it does is make you work more for the money that it takes to buy it.

It's so easy to buy on impulse. It's so easy to *Buy Now and Pay Later*. But when you buy all the stuff, all you're left with is a lack of money and a bunch of clutter. Say no to frivolous purchases. Say no to duplicates. Say no to just-in-case items. Say yes to simplicity. Say yes to calmness. Say yes to financial freedom.

Isn't that what we all want? Calmness and joy every day? More stuff will not bring that. More stuff cannot solve your problems. More stuff won't bring peace and relaxation, it will only clutter your mind and bring you angst. There's no responsibility or energy needed to live simply. Clean out a closet and feel how calm you feel afterward and how nice it feels to be able to find the clothes you really want to wear. It's a great feeling.

Freeze Credit

"Protection from an online hassle is so important in today's society." -Stephanie Aldrich

I have first-hand experience in this area. Two years ago, someone snagged my personal information and started opening credit cards and checking and savings accounts in my name. I filed a police report and went online to TransUnion, Experian, and Equifax, started an account and within a few minutes, froze my credit. It's a very easy thing to do. The criminals proceeded to attempt to open more accounts, but because I had frozen my credit, they were turned down for the accounts and finally gave up on me and moved on.

But their efforts did ding my credit badly and took over two years to bring back to a normal score. I went from 820 to 695 in an instant. Currently, I'm not using my credit for anything as I save and pay cash for what I want to buy, but it's always a good thing to know that I have it if I need it.

It's easy to freeze it once your bureau accounts are set up and it takes seconds to unfreeze them if you're looking to borrow money (which of course I'm discouraging you from doing). This small thing will help keep your identity safer from the criminals that are online trying to make a quick buck on your dime.

Myth of Overnight Success

"Rome wasn't built in a day."
-John Heywood

Social media leads us to believe that if you buy this course, or do this one thing, you'll be famous and rich overnight. Wealthy people know better. It takes a lot of time, patience, energy, and strategy to build wealth. Anyone can look rich by driving a fancy car or going on an extravagant vacation. But what's their net worth? What does their financial statement look like? Are they up to their eyeballs in debt? Are they stressed out because they owe everyone money?

If you want to truly build wealth, you must focus all your energy and attention on doing the right things with your money. That's creating a budget. That's knowing exactly where your money is coming from and where it's going. That's only spending on necessities. That's saving as much as you can and investing it into assets that give you cash flow. Then and only then, can you build wealth that will lead to financial freedom for you and your family. Wouldn't it be wonderful to wake up when you want and spend the day the way you want without having to go to work? That's what money can give you- freedom. But don't think that it will happen overnight, because 99% of the time it won't. Be prepared to do the work and spend the time learning how to multiply your money the right way.

Never Pay Retail

"The 11th commandment: Thou Shalt Never Pay Retail."-Gedelstein

Everything has a price, and that price is the value you place on that object. Price is all made up. The marketplace dictates what things cost and what we're willing to pay for them. This includes goods and services. Smart people know how to stretch their dollars to get the most out of them. This includes shopping for deals. This can include everyday products like groceries and personal products to gas and clothes. But they should also include things like insurance and telephone plans, internet providers, and medical care.

There's so many companies and products to choose from but cost shouldn't be the only way you choose your product or provider. It should depend on the value of the results that you get from that product or service. The result always should equal the value that you're receiving and if it's not, then it's time to go shopping for something or someone else. Make it a priority to regularly shop around for goods and services. Never pay for something just because of laziness to shop prices or out of convenience. Building wealth necessitates creating margin in your budget and that only occurs from getting great value for your money.

Talk About Money

"Money is the last taboo. People will talk about their sex lives before they discuss their finances."
-Marvin H. McIntyre

In some cultures, it's considered rude or taboo to talk about money. This is a major reason why money skills aren't taught to children. Because no one talks about it, no one learns about it and how to do it right. It's a shame that it's this way. I think that's changing with the internet and YouTube where people that know about money are speaking openly about it. I, myself, am contributing to the narrative by hosting a weekly show on YouTube called, you guessed it, *Money Habits.* That show was the inspiration for this book.

I want people to start learning and talking openly about money. If we can learn from each other what works and what to avoid, we can all thrive. When we all thrive, we can tackle the wrongs of society with our wealth and not have it handled by only the social elites that seem to be out of touch with the rest of us. We can set up ourselves and our future generations with the knowledge that can help them thrive and lead rich, healthy, and successful lives. But it's so very important that we are talking about money openly and changing our perceptions of wealth and what it means to us and the rest of society. Money is a great thing and should be sought after.

Mindful Spending

"Saving money is not about earning more, it's about spending less."
-Ziad Abdelnour

Being intentional with our money is the only way that we can become financially free. This means that we must control where our money goes. It must be intentional. We must direct funds first into our savings and investing accounts. Then we must pay our bills. Then whatever is left over, we can spend how we want. It must be in that order or else we will never be financially independent and retire. We must stop moving the goalposts as we advance in our careers. We must tell our spouses that our lifestyle must remain where it is today so that we can save and invest for our future. If we keep spending all our raises and promotions, we will never get ahead and will be living like the other 76% of Americans who don't have $1000 in their savings account for an emergency or are living paycheck to paycheck without any leeway. Controlling our lifestyle means controlling how we spend our money. If we prioritize our future, then we will sacrifice our present condition to build that glorious future. This doesn't mean we can have fun today, but it may mean that we need to be mindful of how we're having that fun and how much it's costing our future to have it now. Be aware of where your money is going and prioritize the future.

Delayed Gratification

"Don't give up what you want most for what you want now." -Richard G. Scott

What do you want most in life? Most people want to live a healthy life full of fun times with their family and friends. This is a great life to strive for, but it takes money to make it happen. Technology will always improve. Science will always discover something new. Fashion will always change and update. There will always be something new and different to buy. But buying this thing interferes with living your best life, then that urge to buy that thing should be squished like the giant spider that's hiding in your bathtub. It just doesn't belong in your life. I know it's difficult to pass up the weekend trip with the guys so that you can pay off your debt. I know it's difficult to drive your old Honda when your best friend just bought a brand-new Tesla. I get it. I had $178,000 in student loan debt at 26 and another $350,000 in business loan debt. Ouch! I lived in a modest home and drove my mom's Baretta for a long time until I paid off my debt. If we want financial freedom, if we want to become debt-free, we must delay our wants for another day in the future until we can actually afford to buy those things. It's tough, I know, but I, like so many other people out there, would rather be debt-free and financially independent than working for the "man" until we're 65 or 70. This requires discipline and a plan.

Turn Waste into Wealth

"It's always consoling to know that today's Christmas gifts are tomorrow's garage sales."
-Milton Berle

Isn't that the truth Milton! An easy way to make a few bucks next weekend is to have a yard or garage sale. Or go through your house and find something that you don't want but is still in good shape and sell it on Facebook Marketplace or Offer Up. People are always looking for good deals on used bicycles, used electronics, and used small appliances. Why pay full price when you can buy it at a steep discount?

Turning your waste into wealth does two things, the first is it helps you declutter your house so that you're not tripping over crap that has no use. This helps you keep a tidy and clean house easier and faster. The second thing is that it helps you recoup money that you spent on that thing that you no longer use so that you don't think that it's a waste. You can use this money to pay off debt, save in your emergency fund, or go on that vacation you've been eyeing for some time. Quarterly or yearly, go through your stuff and start selling items that you no longer need. This is especially important if you're moving or relocating to make your move easier and cheaper. Nobody likes moving boxes full of crap that you never intend to use again. Turn your waste into money today!

Network

"Your network is your net worth." -Tim Sanders

Wealthy people know the importance of who they know. They also know the importance of who knows them. Networking allows you to meet people who have the same interests as you do as well as people from different industries and walks of life. Making money is all about developing relationships with people that in turn develop trust. When people know you and trust you, they will buy from you. It's as simple as that. It's very important to talk to your customers about their lives and what problems they're facing. You can then easily create rapport with them that in turn can create connection. When you know what your customers want and need, you can steer your business around them.

Wealthy people also know the importance of following where the money goes. They get to know bankers and venture capitalists. They get to know manufacturers and industry leaders. They get to know rivals and competitors in their space. Their contact list is long and the relationships they build with these people are strong. That's why they succeed. They know what to make, how to make it, and who to make them for. Start talking with people that are in your industry. You never know when a new opportunity will come your way-maybe a higher paying job or a new account.

Side Hustle

"A side hustle is an easy way to turn your skills and hobbies into extra income."-Unknown

Today, inflation is high. Our dollar is losing its purchasing power by the day. Businesses are cutting their workforce to stay profitable in lean times. It's important to have at least one side hustle that can help to provide more income to your bottom line. This could be a small business you run out of your home. This could be a night job where you pick up an extra shift. This could be seasonal work. This could be doing bookkeeping or taxes on the side for other businesses.

Just like diversifying your investments, it's always a good idea to diversify your income too with a side hustle. Sometimes this means that you're working extra to pay off debt. Sometimes this means that you're doing something different because you love it. Sometimes you're doing something that the community needs. No matter what it is, spend a little free time earning another income stream to protect you in difficult economic times. I write books and create content for YouTube videos. I love doing it and it gives me not only some side income, but also purpose. As you get older and your kids are grown, you can fall back on your hobbies and side gigs for socialization and to supplement your retirement nest egg.

Chapter 3

Compelling Money Habits

Now let's dig deeper into habits that are not just beneficial, but compelling practices that draw you in with their undeniable logic and transformative potential. Compelling, in this context, refers to something that captures attention and convinces one of its merits through clear, persuasive arguments or evidence. These are the habits that, once understood and adopted, have a profound and immediate impact on improving your financial situation.

Why focus on compelling habits? Because they are the catalysts for significant change. They are the practices that, when implemented, deliver noticeable improvements in your financial health and personal satisfaction. This chapter explores such dynamic habits as optimizing your returns to align with your freedom number, harnessing the power of tax savings to maximize efficiency, and creating a vision for what your retirement and financial freedom looks like.

Each habit presented in this chapter is backed by both common sense and modern issues, providing a holistic view of their efficacy. You will learn how these habits have not only changed the fortunes of many but how they can be seamlessly integrated into your life. We will guide you through the steps to adopt these habits, making what seems complex surprisingly straightforward. You'll be engaged and inspired as we uncover these compelling money habits that promise not only to enhance your financial well-being but to revolutionize your approach to managing money. Watch the training below.

Avoid Debt

"The borrower is slave to the lender."-Proverbs 22:7

I grew up in a household where if we could make payments on the item we wanted- car, furniture, or even Christmas presents, we would buy them. Remember the layaway policies of the 70s and 80s where you could purchase an item, the store would hold it for you, and you could make payments on it until you paid for it and then you could pick it up? It seemed that no matter what we did, we owed somebody something. Is that how you want to live? You're probably already doing it right now. Credit cards, Buy Now Pay Later, 0% Down. They're all the same. These financial traps were designed to make you spend, spend, and spend more. These companies don't care if you save your money and invest it to build wealth. They want you tied to them for years so when their product breaks and wears out, you'll line up again and buy some more. Profits and bottom lines are all they care about. So, who cares about you? Me. I want you to break the shackles of the payment system and start putting money aside when you want to buy something so that first of all, you really want it, and second, that once you buy it, you're done, and you can continue saving and investing for your future without owing interest payments to someone else. Want a new car? Pay in cash. *But I don't have the money?* Then you must wait until you do.

Invest Consistently

"Time in the market beats timing the market."-Ken Fisher

Every paycheck, invest at least 25%. Every raise, invest at least 50% and have fun with the rest. Anytime you make money, invest part of it. Invest when the market is up. Invest when the market is down. Diversify your investments. That doesn't mean diversifying all your stock holdings into bonds or international stocks, which could be a good thing, but diversify types of investments: stocks, private credit, real estate, physical gold and silver, energy, technology, and businesses. Invest in qualified plans like a 401k, 403b, or Roth IRA. Invest in non-qualified brokerage accounts too. Have an emergency fund in both cash and in a high-yield savings account.

Use compounding interest over time and diversification in different industries and markets to keep your investments growing and multiplying. That's how wealth is built. This is what you teach your children. This is what will build generational wealth. Isn't it time that you start changing your family's destiny? The answer is, yes! Now is the time. Not tomorrow or the next day. Today is the time to start saving and investing in your future. Start today and don't stop! Every time money touches your hands, invest part of it and watch it grow. The sooner, the better.
Start today!

Always Have Dry Powder

"If a window of opportunity appears, don't pull down the shade."
-Tom Peters

Warren Buffett is the classic example of accumulating money until there is an opportunity in the market to buy. He waits and waits until the conditions are right, and the company is right to pounce and make a move. It's like a cat that sees its prey in the near distance. They wait. They watch. They wiggle their butt and then finally make their move and pounce on their victim. Investing and money are the same thing. We must always have some "dry powder" or money in reserve in case an opportunity- good or bad arises. The bad things are what your emergency fund is for. The good things are what your stash of investment cash is for to seize opportunities in the market, maybe a flash crash, or some economic downturn that you can get an edge on others by having some money to invest when stocks or real estate are low and on sale. That's what all the greats do. They wait patiently on the side for the right time and then they make a move into the investment. This doesn't mean that you wait on the sidelines forever. This is another strategy that you can use alongside investing consistently and steadily over time to help build wealth. Build a dry powder fund that you save and save and then deploy only when the timing is right.

Reinvest Dividends

"Do you know the only thing that gives me pleasure? It's to see my dividends coming in."
-John D. Rockefeller

The easiest way to build wealth and exploit compounding interest in your favor is to reinvest your dividends. In many brokerage accounts this is termed the DRIP method. Dividend Reinvestment Plan. When dividends are paid- usually quarterly by the companies in your investments, your brokerage will take that money and buy more investments. This allows your money to start making more money. This is one of the main catalysts for compounding growth over time. You invest money that makes money and in time, that money starts making more money and so forth until you are financially free. Of course there's different ways to accumulate dividends, but this is the simplest and easiest way to build your wealth over time. Make sure your accounts are reinvesting your dividends and watch as your account grows over the next 10, 20, and even 30 years. It takes no effort once it's set up. This is another way that you can automate your wealth accumulation. Set it and forget it and watch as the money you invest multiplies over time. As those stocks appreciate and grow, usually their dividends grow with them which means even more money will accumulate in your accounts.

Asset Allocation

"The difference between success and failure is not which stock you buy or which piece of real estate you buy, it's asset allocation."
-Tony Robbins

We already talked about diversifying your investments into different non-correlated assets such as stocks or bonds (paper), real estate, energy, agriculture, private equity and credit, precious metals, art and collectibles, or debt instruments. There're so many offsets in each of these categories that you can do the research on your own. Another important part of asset allocation is where your money is placed. Is it a taxable brokerage account? Is it a tax-deferred account? Or is it a tax-free account? Tax-deferred accounts are accounts that allow you to invest money without paying taxes on that money today. 401k's, traditional IRA's, SEP and Simple Plans, and 403B's. Tax-free accounts allow you to save using after-tax dollars including Roth IRA, Roth 403B or Roth 401k's. Taxable brokerage accounts offer no tax breaks in the form of deductions for contributions. The allocation is important if you want to retire early as tax-deferred and tax-free accounts have a minimum penalty-free age of 59 ½. So, if you plan on retiring early, having money in cash accounts or taxable brokerage accounts available to spend until you reach 59 ½ is crucial to your early retirement plan. Location matters.

Minimize Taxes

"Nothing is certain except death and taxes."-Benjamin Franklin

There's nothing wrong with paying less tax. That's why the tax code has over 6800 pages, 70% of which are dedicated to loopholes and tax deductions. Along with asset allocation, minimizing taxes can build wealth even faster by using the tax code to your advantage. Most people think that the tax structure will always be changing in the future. This may mean that taxes will go up which can affect the amount of money you have at your disposal during retirement so minimizing the amount of taxes you pay today and in the future are mission critical. Having a good accountant and regular consultations with a financial advisor can help you strategize how to do this. Investing in different asset classes can also have different tax implications. For example, I invest in real estate syndication deals where I pool my money with the investing company, and they buy and manage the real estate and send me monthly cash flow checks. Those monthly cash flow checks are offset by the depreciation from the property that I share with the primary investor. Since 2018, I haven't paid any tax on that monthly cash flow because of the way that real estate is taxed. I do the same thing for my oil syndication deals. So, make sure you know where to invest your money and how it will be taxed when you need it to minimize the amount of tax you pay the government.

Audit Subscriptions

"We realized the best way to monetize content was through a subscription model."-Trip Adler

$30 for a phone plan. $20 for Netflix. $11 for Planet Fitness. $90 for home internet. $139 for Amazon Prime. $50 for Sam's Club. Then there's utilities that get paid every month. It's no wonder Americans are broke. We use our paychecks to pay for monthly subscriptions and yearly memberships. A great rule of thumb is every June and December, we should evaluate our monthly and yearly subscriptions and memberships.

Ask ourselves:

- Are we using this service?
- Do we need this service?
- Is there a cheaper alternative?
- Can we get rid of it for now?

I do this every year and have eliminated a lot of expenses that would otherwise eat up my income. If I want to watch something on Netflix, I only buy it for that month, binge watch it, and get rid of it. That's an easy solution. I pay for my Sam's Club membership through my business so it's a write off. What subscriptions and memberships can you cut back on or even eliminate?

Sinking Funds

"Sinking fund- NOUN- A fancy economic term for saving."-Unknown

My mother taught me about the sinking fund. She used the envelope method. She would get an envelope and write on it what that money was to be used for. Every paycheck, she would put a designated sum of money into it. When it was time to spend it, she had it saved and would throw out the envelope and start another one for another experience or thing to buy. She did this throughout her life. I am carrying on the habit. But I do things a little differently- I use physical cash envelopes and digital cash accounts. I use them for different types of purchases. My physical cash accounts, I use them for fun activities like vacations, concerts, and clothes. My digital bank accounts are used for cars, investments, and business equipment. I love my cash envelopes because they cause me pain to see an empty envelope after I have spent that money. It really makes me think about what I'm spending that money on and if I really want that thing I'm saving up for. It forms a little friction whereas my digital accounts don't- it's all numbers in an account somewhere. Sinking funds are used to help you keep on track with your budget, so you don't overspend. It helps to enforce delayed gratification and eliminate impulse spending that can sidetrack your financial goals. It's easy to save a little bit over time.

Celebrate Financial Milestones

"It's important to indulge in a well-deserved reward that aligns with your budget."-Faster Capital

Celebrating your financial wins helps to keep your motivation high and helps to provide encouragement to continue pursuing your financial goals. The purpose of this book isn't to tell you all the strict and stringent ways of being disciplined with your money and telling you what not to do with it. The purpose of this book is to help you use your money to create the life you truly want to live. Using money as a tool to free your time and energy so you can pursue your purpose is what's important here. Celebrating your milestones along the way is a great way to reward yourself for your hard work and due diligence. It takes a lot of knowledge and discipline to be good with money and to build wealth. As humans, we need motivation to keep up with that discipline and celebrating our accomplishments is one way to do this. Plan a trip. Buy those shoes you've noticed. Buy that car. Meet some friends out for a nice dinner and drinks. Whatever you want to do, plan to do it AFTER you hit your financial goal. It helps make financial goals a game and you look forward to the reward after hitting that goal. It's the prize after the journey. Do something fun or buy something you want when you start building wealth and hit your first step.

Waiting Period

"Patience is not simply the ability to wait- it's how we behave while we're waiting."-Joyce Meyer

Patience really is a virtue when it comes to money. Whether it's practicing delayed gratification on a purchase you want to make in the future with money you've saved in your sinking fund or waiting patiently while your money grows until one day you have reached financial independence. Every aspect of money comes with a slice of patience on the side. Accumulating money takes time. It takes time to grow. It takes time to develop from a skillset. Before making a purchase, ask yourself whether this purchase is necessary first. If it is, did you properly save for it or is this more of an impulse buy? Building wealth requires having a margin of money in your budget to save and invest with. That's the only way it will happen. If you don't save and prioritize your investing first, you'll spend all your money on other things. That doesn't mean that you can't live your life and have fun along the way. It only means that investments and savings come first, then bills, then the rest is money that you can spend how you like. Unfortunately, most people do things differently. They pay their bills first, then they spend what they want on fun things, and then they save and invest whatever is left over. Many times, there's nothing left over and that's why most Americans are broke. Don't be like them. Be patient and invest first!

Have Fun

"Memento mori- remember you will die. Let that determine what you do, say, and think."-Marcus Aurelius

"YOLO," (You only live once) is a common saying of young people. Unfortunately, they've totally missed the boat when it comes to using their youth to their advantage when it comes to building wealth. They don't realize that their $750 monthly car payment could easily cost them $350,000 in the next 30 years. That's a lot of money to be blowing on stupid things. At the age of 20, every $1 they invest can turn into $88 when they retire through the magic of compounding. But compounding only works over time. At some point, invested money starts making money and so on and so forth until finally you're stinking rich!

Living with intention means that you can live life on your terms, however, compromise must be had to keep your wealth building silently in the background. Automating investments help to keep that happening while you can concentrate on having fun and keeping up with your friends. Everyone will die, but you can choose if you die a wealthy person or a popper. It's up to you if you're going to leave a financial legacy to your children or grandchildren or just fainted memories. Choose wisely now so that time can multiply your dreams.

Credit Union

"When you don't have shareholders to appease, you don't take unnecessary risks."-Unknown

Putting your money in a local credit union has many advantages. One is that they typically offer higher savings rates than bigger traditional banks. They are non-profit organizations, so they only lend to members and don't tend to take on riskier lending practices that big institutions need to take in order to always be making profits. They tend to have lower interest rates if you were to borrow money from them to buy a house or especially a car. Credit union members also have a say in how the credit union operates and any profits made are reinvested in the credit union or given to the members through higher interest rates on savings and lower rates on borrowed money. Most credit unions require you to live in the area where it is located. Some require you to be in a certain industry, like the military or teachers' association. This helps the credit unions tailor offers to a certain group of people and manage their risk so that they can maintain control of the company. Your money is not insured by the FDIC but by the NCUA which is specifically for credit unions. I have some money stored in a credit union and have been happy with their services over the last decade. It may be wise to spread out your emergency fund into one of these institutions and try out their services if you need to.

Vision Board

"You don't have to be great to start, but you have to start to be great."-Zig Ziglar

A vision board is simply an image you can create on Canva with images representing the life you want to live. What's your goals? A Mercedes? A condo on the beach? A boat? A European Vacation? A hot spouse? A loving family? Whatever you want in your life, snag photos from online and create a vision for what your life looks like. This is an old technique for manifestation but a very effective one, especially when it pertains to wealth creation. By putting this image on your phone and laptop, you are reminding yourself of your financial goals on a routine basis. This reminder helps you to maintain focus and motivation to create the wealth you need to fund your desires of material goods and experiences. There's no shame in wanting nice things. I want a Mercedes and a European Vacation. I have my vision board on my phone, and I look at it every time I use my phone. It reminds me to keep working hard, saving, and investing for my financial freedom. It is always reminding me of how I want to live my life and what my priorities with my money are. I want financial freedom so I can spend my days doing whatever it is I want without going to work for the money I need to support those desires. Create a vision for yourself and the financial goals you want to hit and look at it every day to keep your goals in sight.

Chapter 4

Overlooked Money Habits

Next, we'll jump into the subtle yet powerful practices that are frequently missed in conventional discussions about financial success. While these habits may not grab headlines, they are essential cogs in the machinery of wealth building, influencing long-term stability and growth.

In exploring these habits, we focus on the foundational behaviors and mental shifts that foster deep-rooted financial resilience. You'll discover the importance of refining everyday practices that seem inconsequential but are pivotal in shaping your financial landscape. From adjusting your mindset to optimizing how you manage time and resources, each habit discussed provides a steppingstone to enhanced financial clarity and control.

This chapter also highlights the art of strategic thinking in finance—how minor adjustments in your approach can lead to major improvements in your economic outcomes. We examine the transformative power of gradual, consistent actions and the impact of perspective shifts on your financial journey. You'll uncover the hidden layers of financial habits that go beyond mere saving and spending. By integrating these understated yet potent practices into your life, you will unlock new dimensions of financial mastery and pave the way for enduring success and prosperity. Watch the training below.

Patience

"Be fearful when others are greedy and be greedy when others are fearful."-Warren Buffett

Investing can induce fear and make the wrong moves if we allow it to happen. What Warren is saying is to spot opportunities in the market when they happen. Be patient. Allow the prices to come to you instead of you chasing them. Many people buy when they hear about a hot stock or see something happening in the market because they don't want to miss out. Again, FOMO kicks in. Warren and Charlie Munger loved to collect cash and just sit and wait for the opportunity to happen. It's like the housing market of 2020-2021. Interest rates were low and people started buying like crazy, oftentimes spending more money than they would otherwise spend because competition for a small number of houses was rampant and people kept driving prices up with their bidding wars. This drove up the entire market, and now that interest rates are higher and prices are higher, it's completely driven people out of the market.

Regular investing can be that way too. Take the emotion out of it by regularly investing no matter what the market is doing. If you want to get in, you can also wait for a pullback (things being on sale) and then jump in. Be cool. Be patient. Allow the market to come to you and don't chase things up and wind-up spending more.

Change

"Money is a terrible master but an excellent servant."
-Phineas Taylor Barnum

Life will change. You'll get promoted. You may move. You may get married. You may get divorced. You may become debt free. You may have a health scare. We never know what curveballs life has in store for us, but one thing is for certain- change is always around the corner. Obviously, it is wise to be ready for change and that includes our money and our money goals. Sometimes we must pause on investing because we have an urgent need for money like a new baby or a house fire. Sometimes we need to ramp up our savings so we can get out of debt fast. No matter what happens, we must be flexible enough to change our money goals and create a new plan so we can hit them. Things break. People get sick. Accidents happen. Having stores of money can help with all these problems. We will all get older and unable to work. Money can help with this change. If we're wise with our spending and we allow our surplus money to grow and multiply, we can head off any situation that money can help to solve if we allow it to do its job. Put it to good use when you need it, but if times are good, invest it and watch it multiply. Being prepared financially for a rough patch can help bring relief to those that heed this advice. It's a good thing to have money around to help us when we need it. Start saving today!

FOMO

"If you instead spend on frivolous things, you're just showing that your pleasures today are more important than your security tomorrow."-Motley Fool

We all need a diet from spending occasionally. Having extra cash is never a bad thing, especially if you're getting your investments and debt headed in the right direction. In America, our whole economy is based on consumerism. Buy this product. Buy this service. Our marketing efforts are based on FOMO (Fear of Missing Out) and insecurity about ourselves. It's okay to participate in the system from time to time. But we must ask ourselves if this thing is going to keep us on track towards our money goals or if it's going to be a waste of money. Most of the time, it's going to be a waste. That's where the process of elimination will come in. We must think of elimination as the process of intentional spending. We must clean out our finances and eliminate the waste. We don't need 5 streaming services. There's no way we're watching all of them continuously. Cut to one or two. We don't need a new car, ours is working fine. We don't need to go on vacation, we just need some time to ourselves and can do this with a staycation. We don't need that new sweater; we have 10 similar ones in our closets. Eliminating frivolous spending helps to keep our focus on what we really want to spend our money on.

Delegation

"Deciding what not to do is just as important as deciding what to do." -Jessica Jackley

Time is money. It's a fact. But have you calculated how much your time is worth? If you're trying to build wealth, every precious moment you're not spending on fun or family could be spent making money. But how much money is your time worth? It's an easy calculation to make. Take your weekly salary and divide it by 40 hours. That gives you your price per hour. Now think about the things you do when you're not at work. Drive. Clean your house. Mow your lawn. Send emails. Pay bills. Cook. Grocery shop. Laundry. If you want to make more money, you must start delegating some or all these other tasks to other people. You can even use technology to do them for you. If your time is worth $50 per hour, and you can spend $5 for grocery pick-up, then you're ahead $45 for that hour you're not spending grocery shopping. The same goes for mowing your lawn. If the neighbor kid can do it for $40, you're still ahead by $10 overall. Great leaders know how to delegate their time and energy so they can spend it on the thing that makes them a superstar. We can do the same thing. Automate and delegate the things that are sucking your time from you so you can spend that time and energy not only making more money, but also doing the things you want to do with the people you want to do them with.

Discipline

"Control your money. Do not let money control you."-Noel Jones

Money can be hard. Saving and investing can be tricky. Getting out of debt can seem overwhelming. Knowing which investment to choose can seem daunting. Here's where discipline comes in. Here's where sacrifice comes in. Here's where doing the hard thing comes in. The best thing about all of it is that you don't worry about making mistakes. All of us will make them. All of us will do something wrong or stupid with our money and we will lose it. The discipline comes into play when it's time to correct the ship and right what has been wronged.

Do something every day to build your wealth. Set up your bills to autopay. Sell something. Learn about a new investment. Pay off a credit card. Work one more hour. Make one more sale. Do something today that will help your money grow. Working on your money every day is discipline. Thinking about it and taking action to make your financial goals come true takes discipline. It takes focus. It takes energy, time, and attention. That's what discipline is all about. Keep your eyes on the prize which is financial freedom and legacy. Doing the hard things so that in the future it becomes the easy thing. Planning and telling your money what to do is what discipline is all about. Aren't you worth it? Isn't your family worth it? Isn't your freedom worth it?

Money Systems

"Money is a good servant, but a bad master."-Francis Bacon

What do you do with your paycheck? Do you pay whatever bills are due this week and then squander the rest? Unfortunately, that's how most people spend their money. They don't have a plan. They don't have a system set up to tell their money where to go. You can't build wealth like that. You must create systems so that the systems control your money, so you don't have to. They're logical. They're calculating. They're automatic. They're not emotional. They set you up on the right path towards wealth creation and financial freedom. So, what's a good system? Yes, creating a budget is a good money system. List out what money is coming in and what money is going out. Automate your bills. Pay off your debt. Save for retirement. All these things will help you create financial freedom. Save a little for fun. Save a little for a rainy day. Save a little for your kids' school supplies. Every paycheck has a purpose. Every paycheck has a list of things that it must do to build your financial freedom. Set up your systems to tell your money where to go. Automate as much of it as possible so your systems work for you and allow your money to grow and multiply so that it can take care of you in the future. Building a future includes building a money system. What's your money system?

Attitude

"Money is only a tool. It will take you wherever you wish, but it will not replace you as the driver."
-Ayn Rand

We all must be the driver of our wealth. To control it. To tell our money what to do and where to go to help us live our lives to the fullest and take care of us when we need it. This can be an overwhelming request at times. It takes a lot of discipline to make this happen over decades of our lives. The main driver of that discipline is our attitude about money and creating wealth for ourselves. It's our attitude that helps us through rough economic cycles when prices are up, stocks are down, and it seems like our money is stagnant. Having a hopeful and positive attitude can help us through the storms.

If you don't have a good attitude about money, guess what? You won't have any! Money loves attention. Money craves it. Others have said she's like a jealous lover that loves attention and will go where she is admired. That's not saying you must spend all your time thinking about it or trying to earn it, but you should definitely think about it and do what you can to create it. Feeling hopeless because you've made money mistakes and are in debt is no way to live. Flip that frown upside down and be hopeful that it will turn around and then get to work making it happen.

Economic Cycles

"Always be buying."-Unknown

The world lives through different economic phases. There's new innovations and excitement where there's growth opportunities and investments go up. Then there's war, and unemployment, and terrible political policies that stagnate the economy and our investments. You will live through many economic cycles. At the time of writing this book, we're seeing the manufacturing industry starting to wane, yet our stock markets are at an all-time high, and interest rates are high. It doesn't make sense. Yet, I'm still buying. I'm still investing. I'm still getting my small piece of the money pie so that over time it can grow and give me freedom. I just made my first purchase of gold and silver, even though they're at record highs. I waited for a pullback and then made a few purchases. I invested in another medical debt contract. I also invested some more in private equity and credit funds. I've started adding cash to my emergency fund as a hedge for poor economic times ahead. I've even started adding cash to my business for the same purpose. Building wealth is the same as playing cards. You've got to know when to hold 'em, and know when to fold 'em. But never not play the game! It's always going to be low or cheap and it's always going to be high or expensive. No matter what- keep investing! Keep building wealth!

Run Your Own Race

"Comparison is the thief of joy."
-Theodore Roosevelt

We can find ourselves jealous of what others have. We see someone driving a Ferrari and wonder to ourselves what they are doing that we're not doing. We drive though fancy neighborhoods and wonder how these people got there. If you've gotten this far, you're already finding out how they got there. They're good with their money. They own assets. They save and invest their money, so it grows. They provide value to others through their products and services. That's how they have a surplus. That's how they have opulence. That's how they have wealth. Now let's look inside. What are you doing to be the same way? We can't be exactly as they are because we must make sense of our own lives. But we too can be good with our money. We too can own assets. We too can save and invest our money, so it grows and multiplies. We too can provide value to others through our products and services whether we own the business or not. We too can lead an extraordinary life, but we've got to control our money and find our own path to wealth. Yes, it will be challenging. Yes, it will require us to try new things and take risks. Yes, it will mean we make mistakes and fail from time to time. But in the end, we must find what kind of life we want to live and use our money to make that life happen.

The Process

"Want to be successful? Commit to a process, not just a goal."
-Nick Sabin

Nick Sabin was one of the best college football coaches in history. He not only was about winning, but he was about the process of winning. He taught his players to ignore the big picture of important games and winning championships. He only wanted them to focus on the smallest things they could do in each play. One small step taken by all the players working together to meet the same goal. They kept their heads down and only focused on their own jobs for each play and they won. Money is the same way in the real world. We must run our own race. We must do the things that will grow our money. We must automate. We must eliminate. We must save and invest. We must grow the money that comes our way so that we can live the life we want and deserve. We can help others. We can free up our time. We can be free of the 9 to 5 job. We can be an example of how to win with money. Winning with money is a process in itself and we must constantly be working at it, so it starts growing on its own without our time and efforts. Once it starts to grow, then it can provide the freedom we're looking for. What are you going to do today to start the money process? Which move are you going to make today that will help you build wealth and create financial freedom?

Take Responsibility

"If you are born poor, it's not your fault. If you die poor, it is."
-Bill Gates

It's so easy to wait for someone to help. It's so easy to complain and play the victim role. *I came from a bad neighborhood. Bob got the promotion instead of me. I couldn't do that. I can't be that way.* All of these are just lies we tell ourselves to avoid taking responsibility for our actions and our wealth creation. This whole book is about learning and implementing the thoughts, feelings, and actions of wealthy people. We live in the Information Age. There's no excuse for us not to be good with money, no matter where we're from or what job we have. As Americans, we all have the freedom to own assets. We all have the freedom to educate ourselves on money. We all can get rich. We can build our networks. We can buy real estate. We can invest in areas that pay us monthly, quarterly, or yearly. But no one is going to ride in on a white horse and save us. We've got to build wealth ourselves. This means we must take responsibility for our own actions. We must save. We must invest. We must be consistent and unemotional when it comes to our money. It's just simple math. Invest 20% of our money over 25-30 years and it will grow exponentially over time, and we will be financially free.

Avoid Busyness

"When everything is a priority, nothing is a priority."
-Simon Fulleringer

Are you being productive or just busy? It's easy to get caught up in mundane tasks like email, laundry, and QuickBooks. But are these activities directly associated with making money? Nope. So why is your schedule full of these mundane tasks when you're supposed to be working? Being productive means that you're moving towards a sale or a new customer that's directly tied to money and wealth. If you're going golfing to meet a prospective new client, that activity is directly tied to money. If you're just golfing with your buddies to blow four hours of time and a few drinks, then that's a waste. Don't go to dinner and spend $400 unless it includes a business prospect. Don't schedule a meeting in your calendar unless it's directly tied to a sale. If you schedule your day full of money-making activities instead of non-money-making activities, you'll find that your commissions and profits will start to increase. I did this in my own practice. I cut down my schedule to just three days a week. But I knew I had enough business for four lazy days. So, I reworked my schedule so that every minute I'm there, it is full of customers needing dental work. And what that did was free up more time for me to spend writing and making YouTube videos about making money. I'm productive.

Refinance

"Why spend more when you can spend less?"-Unknown

It's important to know what interest rates are doing. When interest rates are low, it's important to leverage good debt and buy assets. When interest rates are high, it's important to store cash and wait for opportunities to arise. Look at what interest rates are right now. Are they high or are they low? Look at any debt you may have. Are the interest rates on that debt higher or lower than what the marketplace is offering? If they're higher than the marketplace, now is the time to refinance them. Usually a change between 1-2% is worth refinancing the debt. Refinancing not only will lower your overall payment, but it could lower the term on your debt. Many times, for not that much change in the monthly payment, you may be able to go from a 30-year loan to a 15-year loan. That's a significant drop in the amount of interest that you will end up paying for one of the biggest investments you will pay in your lifetime. That money can be invested in your future or used to improve your lifestyle. You can consolidate either student loans or different credit cards into one personal loan with one payment to help to pay off the debt faster. Time means money, so if you can not only lower the interest rates that you're paying, but also the amount of time it's going to take you to pay it off, then refinancing is your golden ticket to building wealth.

Own Nothing

"Assets are only assets if you don't own them but control them." -Unknown

Own Nothing. If I've ever learned anything about wealth accumulation, it's this. If you are going to build wealth, you must own assets that pay you. This means that if they're in your personal name, you could lose them through litigation. America thrives on litigation and an easy way to avoid it is to put assets in separate trusts and corporations. That way, each individual asset is separated from the others and from you personally. As you accumulate assets, consult with an attorney that specializes in trusts and corporations so that you can shield your assets behind them.

If you own real estate and someone falls in the shower, they can sue you. But they must sue your rental property corporation and not you personally. They can't take your house or your retirement accounts because you've separated all your assets from your name. This can also help to shield your wealth from scammers. Because you control your assets through these shields, they're not public and can't be tied to your name. Build your wealth and be diligent in protecting it through corporate and trust veils. You'll be so happy you did if someone comes after you.

Listen

"The reason why we have two ears and only one mouth is that we may listen more and talk less."-Zeno

To build wealth, you must be good at communication. This means that you must not only make a connection with your client, but you must also be able to solve their problem. How do you know what their problem is if you don't ask and then listen to them tell you? How do you know if your product or service is right for them if you don't shut up and listen to them? You can't. Great communicators and salespeople know that the best way to make money is to communicate with their clients effectively. And this means that they need to make a connection with their clients. They need to get to know them and understand what they need. They must build rapport. They must build trust and that takes time and effort on your part to be a good listener. To increase your income also means that you need to learn new skills. How can you build wealth if you don't throw your ego out the door and listen and learn from someone who knows more than you? Now is the time to make more money and that means you need to take different actions. Take advice and direction for mentors who have the results that you want to get. Especially when it comes to building wealth and financial freedom. Listen more and implement what you've heard.

Mistakes

"The only real mistake is the one from which we learn nothing."
-Henry Ford

Everyone makes mistakes, especially with money. We've all made stupid decisions with our money. That's why you got this book, to learn better money habits. Sometimes the market will go sour, and you lose business and investments. Be patient, it will turn around. Sometimes you put your money in a high yield savings account and three months later, the interest rate plummets and it's not worth saving it there anymore. Sometimes you invest in a rental property only to have the market bust a few years later. If you are patient and allow the market to correct itself, you won't lose a lot of money. Sometimes you will have to pivot with your investment strategy. Sometimes you will have to take a lower-paying job to learn new skills that will get you a promotion down the line. Sometimes a business will fail that you put money into. It's okay. It happens. You've come so far in your wealth creation journey that a little failure now and then won't set you into a tailspin. Redirect your attention in a different direction when a failure occurs. Learn from your mistakes and find a better solution. Don't be afraid to fail at something new, you're young and still have time to correct the mistake. Fail fast and get back into the game.

Ask

"The greatest gift is not being afraid to question."-Ruby Dee

You don't know something-ask. Ask for help. Ask for answers to your problems, confusion, and doubt. When you don't know something, ask someone who does. Building wealth and living a fulfilled life isn't easy. But you don't have to figure all of it out on your own. Others are doing *exactly* what you want to do and are living the life you want to live. So, ask them how they're doing it. *Ask and ye shall receive.* I tell my son every day before school- ask good questions. I don't want him to be afraid to ask the teacher to explain something to him if he doesn't know the answer. Sometimes we feel shame because we don't know the answer. So what? That's why we're there, to learn and improve our situation. Ask! No question is dumb. If you want a promotion at work, ask your boss how you can contribute more. Ask him what skills you need to learn and improve. Ask her who you need to connect with. Ask what you must do to help the team more. If you want to start investing in real estate, find a mentor that's doing it, and ask them questions. Follow their processes. Take action. When you're stumped, ask for help. Asking is one of the most powerful things you can do to build wealth. It means that you're willing to learn something new and to set your ego aside. When in doubt, just ask!

Chapter 5

Timeless Money Habits

We now come to enduring practices that have stood the test of time, providing value and stability through generations. These habits draw on the wisdom of simpler times and integrate them seamlessly into the modern financial landscape, offering a blend of nostalgia and practicality that can enhance today's sophisticated economic life.

In this exploration, we uncover the principles and behaviors that have consistently contributed to financial success. These practices are not bound by time or trend but are rooted in fundamental financial wisdom that applies universally. From the art of living within one's means to the disciplined pursuit of saving and investing, each habit discussed here has been a key driver of financial security and prosperity through the ages.

As we navigate through these timeless habits, you'll learn how to apply age-old wisdom in a modern context, enhancing your financial strategy with proven methods of managing and growing wealth. This chapter encourages a return to the basics, emphasizing the importance of adopting straightforward yet powerful habits that are often overshadowed by more complex financial strategies.

You will be able to strengthen your financial foundations by embracing these time-tested practices. By incorporating these habits into your daily life, you will build a robust financial portfolio that is both resilient and capable of weathering economic fluctuations. Watch the training below.

Barter

"The rule of bartering is that the transaction equally benefits both parties."-Unknown

Bartering has been around for thousands of years. It was around before our money system, and it will be around afterwards. Why not use this ancient method of trade? Especially when it benefits both parties. I have gotten a lot of work done to my house- electric wiring, plumbing, drywall, and deck construction through bartering with others. I, as a dentist, have something they need, and they know how to do things I need. It's a win-win situation.

Another aspect of bartering and trading is that of taxes. Time is always money, but you can spend your time bartering and trading with someone else and that kind of time isn't taxed. If no money is exchanged through your businesses, then no tax event has occurred, and the government can't get their greedy hands on your transaction. This is a beautiful thing! Whether you own a business or not, you can trade your time and skills with someone else and you both can benefit greatly. This is how communities were built in the past and should be run today. We're so caught up with making more money that we forget that we can help one another solve the problems we have simply by bartering and trading our skills and talents with those around us.

Plant a Garden

"To plant a garden is to believe in tomorrow."-Audrey Hepburn

Anyone can plant a garden- even those that are living in apartments. All you need is a small planter, some dirt, and a plant, and viola- you're a gardener. For people that have a backyard, you can easily grow tomatoes, peppers, zucchini, and squash in any amount of dirt. Planting a garden not only helps you save money at the grocery store, but it also helps you control your own food supply. I have had a garden for over a decade and have made a lot of sauce, salsa, and muffins from my garden. I've grilled many, many side dishes from my garden.

The best book I ever read was about square foot gardening. They talk about how to get the most use out of the space that you have as well as how to condition the soil the right way to be able to grow a variety of different plants. If you have the right soil and some sunshine, anyone can supply their families with delicious, chemical-free vegetables throughout the late summer, early fall seasons. To keep the critters out, you can fence in your garden. I have a wooden fence around mine and don't have any issues with the wildlife feasting on my hard work. If you want to save some money during the summer and feed your family delicious veggies, plant a garden in the spring as soon as the frost goes away.

Multi-Generational Living

"Blood makes you related, love makes you a family."-Unknown

In many cultures, multi generations live together. It is very common to Asian, African, Latin American, and Middle Eastern families, even here in America. In Indian households, it is common to have the parents move in with the oldest son when he gets married and pass the home onto him upon their death. This helps to reduce household expenses and provides childcare to the younger generations while the parents go off to work.

Sometimes young adults just getting out of college need to live with their parents for stability until they break out into the job market and start making it on their own. Sometimes a parent moves back in with one of their children to help take care of them both physically and financially if another parent has passed away. In today's high-interest and high-priced housing market, I think you're going to see more and more of this occur in the United States because it's going to be harder and harder to find good priced housing for the younger generations to buy and will be more affordable to either rent or live with their parents or another sibling. It just makes good financial sense if you can live with your mom or mother-in-law as an adult.

Canning

"Waste not, want not."-Unknown

Canning and preserving food at home is a way to extend its shelf life. Before refrigeration, canning was used to keep sauces, jams, and vegetables preserved during winter months to provide food when the crops were barren. And of course, it's still used today. I personally don't can anything, I think it's a tedious process that if not done right, will end up making everyone sick. But it still is a method that can help you save not only money on food, but also time during the winter months preparing meals. What I do is freeze the things that I grow. I make sauce and salsa. I make zucchini muffins that freeze well. The rest of my garden I eat fresh during the summer and fall months.

You can make some good money at farmers' markets if you can your salsas, jams, and sauces. There's a high demand for fresh food that's homegrown and without preservatives and all the chemicals that modern factories put in our food supply. The money you make from your canning can help to build your retirement fund, pay for your kid's college, or even next year's vacation. These farmer's markets are easy places to network and meet new people that could potentially be new clients in your 9-5 job. So not only can your canning help you preserve nutritious food, but it can also help you grow your wealth.

Mend and Repair

"The time to repair the roof is when the sun is shining."-John F Kennedy

There's a lost art form in America- and that's to mend and repair things. We're not taught to fix anything anymore. We're taught to hire someone to do it for us, like we're some type of useless royal. If we want to build wealth and reach financial independence, we must increase our skill sets and this includes learning how to fix stuff. We have a wonderful ally in the learning process- that's YouTube! You can find a YouTube video on just about anything nowadays. Maybe your dryer is throwing an error code. More than likely it's a faulty $50 part that you can fix yourself by following along on a video. Maybe your headlight on your car is out and instead of paying a mechanic $300 to fix it, you can fix it for under $100 by watching a video and following their instructions. There's millions and millions of videos on YouTube that give instructions on how to fix stuff. All you must do is search for it. Over time this could save you thousands and thousands of dollars that could be used to invest in your own wealth. Stop paying someone else to fix your stuff and make at least an attempt to fix it yourself. You'll get it down quicker and cheaper than waiting around for someone else to fix it for you.

Homemade

"My favorite things often have a story behind them and are usually handmade."-Amy Sedaris

The smell of freshly baked cookies or bread. The feel of a crocheted blanket from Grandma. The taste of freshly made sauce out of the garden. The coolness of a personally designed T Shirt. All these things are handmade. All these things take skill. All these things are made from love. We need to keep these traditions alive in America. Things our grandmothers did for us. Skills our grandfathers had that made things special. It's so nice to receive something homemade. It tastes better. It smells better. It feels better. And when we think about the effort and skill that went into making it, it warms our hearts. They were thinking about us. They were making it for us because they thought we'd love it. That's what homemade things are about. It saves money. It saves time. It also creates connections between people. It helps bring them together to create something special. Baking a fresh loaf of bread costs pennies but the way it makes us feel is priceless. We don't use preservatives. We eat it when it's still warm. We don't have to go out of the house to enjoy it. We know what's in it. This is what making things is about. Controlling what goes into it and the result. Don't knock Etsy or the farmers' markets or the local craft shows. That's where genius and connection are made. That's truly priceless.

Natural Remedies

"Plants have spirit, and that spirit is the strongest medicine."
-Elliot Cowan

We can get sick. We can get run down. We have aches and pains. Science is a wonderful thing in that they spend millions and millions of dollars on researching new treatments for what ails us. But there's also side effects that come from these engineered drugs and people should be cautious when taking anything that has more side effects than the ailment must begin with. That's where natural remedies come into play. There are many plants that have natural chemicals in them that can help us feel better. The Chinese have been making herbal medicinal teas for centuries. Aloe helps to heal the skin. Turmeric and cherries can decrease inflammation. Honey can help with a sore throat. Clove oil can soothe an achy tooth. Ginger can help with digestion. Apple cider vinegar can help calm down indigestion and heartburn. Garlic can help with high blood pressure. Echinacea can help with skin outbreaks. Chamomile tea can calm the nerves and help you fall asleep. Ginseng can help boost your brain function. Peppermint can help with congestion. Lavender can calm down anxiety and help you fall asleep. Ginko can help with memory. Primrose oil can help with PMS. Flaxseeds can help lower blood pressure. Tea tree oil is good for athlete's foot and toe fungus. Try natural remedies first- they're cheaper and prevalent.

Carpool

"Share the ride, share the joy."
-Brandboy

Carpooling is an effective way to not only save the planet from carbon emissions, but also can save you money in the process. In areas of heavy traffic, it's nice to not have to stress out about it. On long commutes, it's nice to sit back and catch up on a podcast or some emails that have been in the background. With other kids, it's nice to relieve other parents that may not have the time or the convenience of dropping their kids off to practice. No matter your circumstance, carpooling can help with time, energy, and certainly money. It can create connections with others that have the same purpose. This can always lead to networking opportunities that may not be available without these special connections. Saving on the wear and tear on your car as well as gas costs can help you save money so you can invest more and build your wealth. It's a good feeling when you can pool your resources with others for a common result. Saving time, energy, and money not only helps you, but also the other people that are doing the same thing. If you're in a big city or are involved with sports locally, consider starting or joining a carpooling or share ride program. You can even start one yourself, knowing that it can help others save money and build wealth.

Potluck

"To be successful, you can't just show up to the potluck with just a fork."-Dave Liniger

Potlucks are about sharing. They're about giving. They're about building community. It's an easy way to connect with others over a good meal. Many cultures gather around a table of homemade food. Potlucks are the same. It's an easy excuse to get together with friends and family you love and want to spend more time with. Instead of slaving in the kitchen all day, potlucks give the host or hostess the time and energy to interact with his or her guests. Sharing the burden and costs of providing food to others helps to make potlucks an ultimate community activity.

It's not only about the yummy food. It's also about the rekindled connections with friends and family. It's also about sharing a beautiful night together. It's also about creating memories and lasting bonds. Potlucks can be held on the coldest day in January or the sunniest day in July. No matter what time of year it is, plan a potluck with your friends or family. Have everyone bring something to the party and celebrate life over good food together. You'll be so glad you did.

Community Resources

"Alone we can do so little, together we can do so much."-Helen Keller

Every community has parks that hold sporting events, community events, as well as provide a place to picnic or exercise. What about libraries? Libraries often loan out equipment, instruments, or tools that can help spark your inner entrepreneur. I can't tell you how many books, magazines, and audiobooks I have absorbed for free from the Libby and Hoopla apps on my phone. Then there's community events. There's always something to do in big cities and suburbs. There are block parties. There are art festivals. There's band stands and bake sales. There's food and cultural celebration festivals. Then there's also volunteer gatherings to build houses, adopt pets, and even feed the homeless. There's kids' events, senior events, LGBTQ events, and everything in between. No matter what community you live in, there's always an opportunity to not only help each other but also to be entertained without spending a lot of money. Community gatherings are an easy way to connect and network with neighbors. It's a time to build healthy relationships. It's a time to have fun with each other. It's time to work on a common goal. Look online and find an event near you. Go out and have some good food, listen to good music and interact with others from your neighborhood. Enjoy the nice weather with your family.

Borrow

"If you got it full, return it full."-Unknown

One of the oldest neighborhood traditions comes in the form of borrowing and lending. But there's rules when borrowing and lending tools and equipment:

1. To lend is to help. Make sure the tool or equipment is in perfect working order so the borrower can use it properly.
2. There's an expectation from the lender to the borrower that their tool or equipment will be returned in the same shape as when they lent it out.
3. There should be a clearly defined timeframe in which the tool or equipment can be used so that life doesn't get in the way of the project at hand and the tool or equipment gets tossed aside and not used.
4. There's also an expectation that the tool or equipment will be returned in working order if it is lent in working order. If it breaks or doesn't work, an equivalent replacement must be purchased and given to the lender for their generosity and to make things right.

Wake Up Early

"Early to bed, early to rise makes a man healthy, wealthy, and wise." -Benjamin Franklin

There's something special that comes with waking up early. I have found that over the years, I treasure waking up early before everyone else. I can think clearly. I'm fully rested and have my biggest creative breakthroughs in the early morning. This book and every book I've ever written were written before 7am. There are no distractions. There's no chaos. There are no interruptions. It's just me and my thoughts. I can enjoy the sunrise. I can enjoy my cup of tea. I can fill my mind with a spiritual podcast or video. Early morning is a special quiet time that everyone should explore each day.

Most CEO's and wealthy people get up around 5am- they're part of the 5am club. This is the time that they work on themselves by exercising and doing their mental work. They also spend this time getting ready for their day, planning their schedule and their flow work. They give themselves several hours during the day that they're most productive, working on solving problems that will make a difference in their companies which will drive up profits and help build wealth. Use these wee hours of the morning to build your day and your wealth too.

Silver and Gold

"Gold is the money of kings, silver is the money of gentlemen, barter is the money of peasants, and debt is the money of slaves."-Norm Franz

I never knew why people would save silver and gold until I finally figured out our fiat money system. The central banks create money with the click of a button. It's not backed by gold or by our GDP numbers, they just create it out of thin air. What that does is it makes the money that's already out in the system less valuable. That's what inflation is. The $20 bill in our wallet still looks like a $20 bill from 10 years ago, but what it can buy is less over time. That's inflation. So, throughout this book, I've talked about the way in which you can invest money in assets that pay you in cash flow and value. But you also must have money in your emergency fund in case something goes wrong. Does that all have to be in cash that is going down in value over time? Nope. An idea to grow your emergency fund is to have some of it as silver and gold. As of 2024, both have been gaining momentum. Silver's supply is being eaten up by demand for batteries and electronics. Gold is just as hard to find and is being hoarded by central banks around the globe. What do they know that we don't know? These metals have been valuable for thousands of years. Yes, they don't give off cash flow, but they do grow in value over time.

Sunday Dinner

"Food is our common ground, a universal experience."-James Beard

Sunday dinner is a solid money habit. Why? Because it strengthens bonds between your family members. When you have a strong family, you feel support when you go out and battle the outside world. You feel energy. You feel courage. You feel free to pursue your dreams and goals. It's like a springboard that allows you to leapfrog over your competition. It's like a burst of energy to go the extra mile to finish your project or make one more sale. When someone has your back (your family) you feel invincible and that feeling alone will make you wealthy. Sunday dinner is almost a lost art. Unless you have an Italian grandmother, gathering around the table for a big Sunday night meal is almost unheard of in today's culture. As mentioned previously, this is a shame. If you have an extended family that lives in your area, start this important ritual this week. Start building that strong foundation of support that you can use to shield you from your daily obstacles and enjoy good food and conversation with those that love you the most. Security and safety is where creativity can thrive. Creativity is where money is made. Discuss social issues and bounce money-making ideas on your relatives. Debate money principles and pass on the ones that resonate with you from this book to help your family tree thrive.

Pay in Cash

"Price is what you pay. Value is what you get."-Warren Buffett

Paying in cash does two things. One, it keeps the government from digitalizing the dollar and controlling the money supply. Two, it hurts a little. I love paying in cash. It helps me stay on budget and makes me rethink any impulse buying that I may want to do. I save most of my discretionary income in cash envelopes that I then spend on that particular item or experience. As I'm writing this book, I just deposited money from a cash envelope into my debit account so I could see a concert. This action stops me from spending money I don't have. It's so simple to just swipe your credit card. This simple gesture is responsible for over $1,000,000,000 or one trillion dollars in debt. That's a lot of zeros. Paying in cash helps to keep our behaviors and our wants in check. Feeling that paper leave your hands is like taking candy from a child- it hurts a little.

If you don't like physical cash, then use a debit card. It's the same thing. You must have the money in your account to use it. This creates friction when it's Friday night and you're bored and decide to browse Amazon. If you only have your debit card linked to your account, you'll think twice about buying that shirt that's on a limited time deal. Paying in cash or debit can significantly tame your shopping habit if you have one.

Chapter 6

Recession-Proof Money Habits

Economic downturns are an inevitable part of financial life, but being well-prepared can significantly mitigate their impact. This chapter focuses on creating lasting habits that fortify your financial health against the unpredictability of recessions, ensuring that your finances remain stable even in turbulent times.

Here, we explore a series of strategic behaviors and mindsets that are essential for weathering economic storms. From building and maintaining an ample emergency fund to diversifying income sources, the habits discussed in this chapter are designed to bolster your economic resilience. We dive into the importance of staying informed about financial markets, understanding the economic indicators that precede downturns, and adjusting your financial plans accordingly.

Moreover, this chapter emphasizes the value of flexibility in financial planning, encouraging adaptive strategies that can respond dynamically to changing economic landscapes. You'll learn how to scrutinize your expenses, prioritize essential spending, and maintain a lean financial profile that can adapt as circumstances evolve.

Recession-proof habits are not just about survival; they are about thriving in any economic environment. By the end of this chapter, you will be equipped with the tools to not only protect your assets during a downturn but also to identify and seize opportunities that recessions can present. Watch the training below.

Job Security

"If you truly want job security, don't count on others, count on yourself."-Frank Sonnenberg

Economies are boom or bust. Businesses are booming or bust. There are times to make a lot of money, and there's times to hoard it and wait for an opportunity. During a recession it is very important to make yourself indispensable. What does being indispensable mean? That means when it's time to start laying off people, they look over you because they don't want to lose you and your skill sets. They know that you are the person that can help them through the recession. But what does this mean? What skills do you have to have? No matter what industry you're in, you've got to become a better communicator. You've got to become good at sales, good at initiating contact with others, and good at following up. You've got to be the number one salesperson. You've got to be the number one project leader. You've got to be the number one manager. You've got to be able to inspire others to be more productive. You've got to be creative and find ways of making your company more efficient. You've got to become a leader whose ideas matter and whose ideas bring in more revenue to the company. You've got to put in more effort than those around you and show others that you're here to stay. If you do this, they'll pass you by when it's time to give others the pink slips.

Preventative Healthcare

"An ounce of prevention is worth a pound of cure."-Benjamin Franklin

Your health is very important. You can't build wealth if you're sick. Today is the time to look at what you're doing with your health and change the bad things that don't serve you. You must be well rested. Sleep is the number one thing that can hinder your health. You must eat correctly. A low carb, high protein diet can help you lose weight and increase your energy so that you can not only have more fun with your family and friends, but also do the things that we've been talking about throughout this book to make more money and build wealth. Making money and building wealth takes a lot of energy and mental clarity. If you have brain fog, if you're tired, or if you're worn down, you can allow emotional and outside triggers to affect your financial decisions. Supplement where needed. Exercise. Take up a physical hobby that you enjoy. Walk. Meditate. Clear your mind of nonsense that always seems to clutter your spirit. If you start taking care of yourself now, you'll have so much more time on this Earth to do the things you want to do and enjoy your family and friends. Do the hard things today so that they will help to take care of your body as you age. Go to bed early. Wake up early and start moving your body and get the blood flowing.

DIY

"It takes half your life before you discover life is a do-it-yourself project."-Napoleon Hill

Wow! This quote is so true. Not only do we have to learn how to build relationships and take care of our health as we've discussed earlier, but we also must learn how to build wealth for ourselves and those around us. This includes saving money where we can to invest it in other areas. This means that we must learn everyday skills and not-so-common skills that can help us navigate life's journey. Everything will break. Everything will wear. Everything will get a hole in it. Everything will get old. So, what will you do about it? Yes, we must learn how to fix stuff. We must learn how to make things new again. We must learn how to renovate. Car maintenance. Home repair and renovation can be very expensive if you don't know how to do it. YouTube is a great source of knowledge for those of us that want to save money and learn a lifetime valuable skill at the same time. I learned how to mud drywall by watching a series of YouTube videos and that has saved us thousands and thousands of dollars in home renovation. Learn to sew. Learn to cook. Inflation has made eating out, even at fast food restaurants, a luxury, so learning how to make nutritious meals at home has become an essential skill. Get off your butt and go learn how to do something to fix something.

Adaptability

"The art of life lies in a constant readjustment to our surroundings."
-Okakura Kakuzo

Building wealth is not a straight line. Neither is success. There's dips and swerves and obstacles in the way. There's market crashes and wars and layoffs at work. Interest rates go up, interest rates go down. The economy booms, and everyone is buying from you and the economy crashes, and no one is buying. No matter what the outside environment is, you've got to remain strong on the inside. You've got to be adaptable to whatever comes your way. Your kid falls off his bike and breaks his arm. You've prepared with an emergency fund, so any hospital bills can be paid. The market crashes and your retirement accounts are down by 30%. You know that this means that these stocks are on sale, and you decide to buy more shares. You know you didn't lose any shares, they're just not worth as much so you buy more to add to your number of shares. Being flexible and mentally adaptable is a must to build long lasting wealth. The wants and needs of the marketplace change. You've got to change your messaging and the products and services so you can serve them properly and make money. Certain investments fall out of favor while others become hot and the future. You must be not only adaptable but also resilient to make different decisions that will continue your financial journey towards building wealth.

Needs vs Wants

"You can't always get what you want, but if you try sometimes, you might find, you get what you need." -The Rolling Stones

To be recession-proof it's essential to figure out what is considered a want and what's considered a need. Everyone needs food. Everyone needs shelter. Everyone needs clothes. Everyone needs money. But what kind of food? What kind of shelter? What kind of clothes? How much money? To build wealth, we need extra money in our budgets to save it and invest it to grow in the future. So, we've got to really dial in our wants and needs to have that margin to secure our finances in turbulent times. When the economy goes bust, as it does from time to time, it's essential for us to be ready to protect ourselves and our investments. It's important to live more frugally and simply to not be harmed by supply chain interruptions and product shortages. It's important to conserve our energy and time. It's important to conserve our spending habits. It's important to conserve our food and home supplies. When we learn what basics meet our needs, then we can splurge a little on the other things when times are great. Then we know we'll be alright when times aren't that great. Have the basics down pat: an extra freezer with food, extra water, a generator, cash, and a firearm with ammo in case things go wrong.

Recession

"I'm living my life, not buying a lifestyle."-Barbara Kruger

78% of Americans are living paycheck to paycheck. They're caught in this never-ending saga of keeping up with their friends. They see the constant ads on Instagram and TikTok about all the latest gadgets and potions that can make them more fulfilled and happier. They see all their friends buying these gadgets and potions and being suckered by the marketing manipulators and influencers on social media. But when shit hits the fan, people will start waking up. I'm writing this in the summer of 2024, the stock market is at an all-time high, but if you really dig into things, it's being manipulated to go higher and is not based on solid economic trends. Inflation is high. The Cost of goods is high. Gas is high. People aren't spending money on frivolous goods because they've realized they're maxed out on their credit cards and there's massive layoffs happening. So what should you do in this environment? Buckle down and only spend money on things that really make you happy. If you want Starbucks coffee, okay, but you can't spend that money on new skincare too. You've got to choose where you spend your money because you must also be putting money away for bad times that might be happening all around you. Choose the places that matter to you and spend your money on those areas and forget the rest. Economic downturns happen, protect yourself ahead of time.

Optimize Insurance

"You don't buy life insurance because you are going to die, but because those you love are going to live."-Unknown

We're all going to die. That's 100% certain. Sorry for spoiling your day. 5.2 million car collisions happen yearly. 7.9% of the population have overnight stays at the hospital. What this means is that we must protect our wallets in case of emergencies by optimizing our insurance plans. This also means that we should be seeking the best coverage for the best price every year. I had a patient that worked for an insurance company, so I went with him for about 20 years. When we had a huge storm and our roof was damaged, the insurance company denied our claim even though 8 houses around us got new roofs because of the hail damage. I immediately canceled my policy and searched for another insurance company. I had another patient who was an independent agent and after that, we have gotten better coverage for less cost on all my needs. My independent agent shops around twice a year and I am happy about the results that I have achieved. My advice to you is to make sure you are buying insurance for all your needs through independent agents who are looking out for you and your wallet. They're not married to any company and will always help you solve your insurance issues with a quick phone call and photo. Make sure you protect yourself in case of emergencies.

Update Resume

"Strive not to be a success, but rather to be of value."
-Albert Einstein

When the economy is shaky, it's a good thing to prepare for a move. Keep your resume updated and always be looking for the next step of the ladder to climb. This doesn't mean that you'll make a move, but it's always a good thing to be on the offensive side of employment rather than the defensive side. I've never had to worry about a job as I've always owned my business. But I can tell you that growing up my father wasn't as fortunate. He ended up being laid off many times throughout his career and ended up owning his own business that he ended up selling and retiring at the end of his career.

Pursue LinkedIn connections as an easy way to remain in the forefront of potential employer's minds. Building wealth requires a constant stream of money flowing into your investment accounts. If you're laid off because of a recession, this will cut off that flow of income and will damage your path to financial freedom and wealth accumulation. Quickly take advantage of all job opportunities that come your way. When there's an opportunity for advancement, grab it and invest most of the surplus in your retirement accounts to help your nest egg grow even faster.

Avoid Panic

"I will tell you the secret to getting rich on Wall Street. Be greedy when others are fearful. And be fearful when others are greedy."
- Warren Buffett

Most people get emotional about their money. That's why they don't use cash. When you use cash to pay for things, there's pain in giving it physically to someone else. This makes us think more about what we're spending that paper on. When we spend money using a credit card, we don't feel that pain. How do you feel when the stock market goes down and your account is worth less this week than last week? Do you panic? Do you get angry? Do you want to just sell everything and sit on the sidelines until the market levels out? Money isn't emotional. Being wealthy is not emotional. Money is neutral. Wealth is neutral. They're both just math equations. Putting a lid on your money emotions can help keep you on course to your freedom number. Thinking logically and being knowledgeable about how markets work and how economic cycles affect them can help guide you towards your financial freedom. Wealthy people know when to stay on the sidelines. They also know that when people are panicking, there's hundreds of opportunities in the marketplace to make more money. So, what type of person are you going to be? Are you going to be emotional or are you going to stay level-headed?

Food Saver

"No one likes to eat freezer-burnt food."-Unknown

During lean times, it's important not to waste anything and this includes food. Buying your food in bulk and vacuum sealing it in portions then freezing it will help you to ensure that your food stays as fresh as possible. I cook a lot of protein on my grill and then portion them out into separate bags, vacuum seal them, and then store them in the freezer for a later date. This not only saves me money because I buy in bulk at a lower prep cost, but it also saves me time because I've prepared my meals ahead of time. When you're busy at work all day, the last thing you want to do when you get home is prepare dinner. A food saver can help you prepare food ahead of time. Then you can freeze it and thaw it out when you need it.

40% of food that's produced, processed, and transported in the United States ends up in a landfill. Wasted food is a drain on our natural resources, our wallets, and our communities. It's important when we're building our nest eggs, not to waste our money. This includes food that's not being used to fuel our bodies. Invest in a Food saver and a freezer and stock up on proteins when they go on sale. It's smart and makes meal prep more convenient.

Prepared Mindset

"Be prepared."-Motto of the U.S. Boy Scouts

We live in a dualistic world. Up and down. Left and right. In and out. Money flows the same way- in and out of our lives. The economy goes through cycles, up and down, and we must prepare for the down turns when it's in a boom. Most people don't do this. They think ignorantly that boom times will always be boom times and they end up getting clobbered financially when things go the other way. There's a simple solution to this: be prepared. This means that you're doing as many things that I've listed in this book as possible. You're always looking for more income streams. You're always working on your network and your skill sets. You're always controlling your spending, even in good times, and saving and investing as much as you can for the future. You're saving cash on the side to take advantage of a downturn. You're cooking at home and building strong family relationships. You're teaching your children about money and how it works. You are reviewing your investments and tweaking them when necessary. You're making sure your estate planning and insurance are up to date and relevant. You're taking care of your health and spirituality. You're doing everything you can to live the best life you can, no matter what's happening in the outside world. But you're also preparing your environment for what could go wrong and having the wherewithal just in case.

Chapter 7

Happy Money Habits

Now it's time to shift our focus from the mechanics of money management to the joy it can bring into our lives. Money, often seen as a source of stress, also holds the incredible potential to enhance our happiness when used thoughtfully and intentionally. Here, we explore the habits that not only optimize financial health but also maximize personal satisfaction and well-being.

This chapter justifies the practices that make financial management enjoyable and fulfilling. From investing in experiences that enrich our lives to supporting causes and communities we care about, the habits discussed here demonstrate how money can be a tool for creating positive change and personal happiness. You'll learn how spending money on others can boost your mood, how planning for future fun can enhance your anticipation and enjoyment, and how using money to foster personal growth and hobbies can be deeply rewarding.

Moreover, we discuss the balance of spending and saving in ways that maintain financial security while allowing for joyful expenditures. By integrating these happy money habits into your life, you can transform the way you perceive and interact with your finances. Instead of viewing money management as a chore or a source of anxiety, these practices help you see it as an avenue for joy and a means to build a richer, more satisfying life.

It's time to embrace a new perspective on personal finance, one where money is not just a necessity but a contributor to your happiness. By the end of this chapter, you'll be equipped with strategies to make your financial activities a source of joy and contentment. Watch the training below.

Enough

"It is not one who has little, but one who craves more, who is poor."
-Seneca

At some point, you will have to decide on what the final number for you is. Then once you hit that number, you must be satisfied with the results. You must be happy with that number and not seek more. This is a tricky situation that must be resolved. As we get older, our situation changes. We have families and usually increase our lifestyles. At some point, we must realize what is important to us, more stuff or freedom. When we realize that freedom is the ultimate reward, then we can start cutting back on the stuff that doesn't matter to us and settle on a number that we can work for and achieve that will give us the freedom that we desire. Usually, you realize that number by 40. Currently, you notice the kids are growing up and doing their own thing. You also notice that you're busier than you've ever been. And you also notice that you're more tired than you've ever been. Maybe you're out of shape. Maybe you're starting to have health issues. At this point, it's important to set a final number to hit and then track your progress towards that number. Don't move the goal post. Be satisfied with what you've accomplished and put your effort into hitting that number so that you can enjoy the rest of your life free from working for your money. Allow your money to work for you. This is the true meaning of enough.

Charity

"Always give without remembering and always receive without forgetting." -Brian Tracy

A fun way to spend your money is not on yourself but on someone else. Charity doesn't have to be this boxed in thing. It could be a large tip to the waitress close to the holidays. A couple of years ago, I treated my son to breakfast at the Waffle House on his first day of Christmas Break. I knew our bill would be under $20. Prior to going, he had written a note to leave that told them to enjoy their holidays. I gave him a $100 bill to leave under our plates and I went up and paid the bill. We left. We watched and saw our waitress clear the table and pick up the money with a huge smile on her face. We'll never forget how that simple gesture could help someone who is not making a lot of money. That's what charity is. Helping. When you've done everything in this book to cut back your spending, to living frugally and spending your money wisely so you can invest it and multiply it over time, you'll find that once you have some extra, you want to help others with it because you know what money has done for your life and you want to help others experience the same thing. Some people tithe a 10th of their salary to their church. Some people give to their local food bank. Others to cancer research. Some to a bake sale. It doesn't matter the size of the donation that's given, it's the feeling that's received once it's given.

Vacations

"The world is a book and those who do not travel read only one page."
-St. Augustine

It is important to rest. It is important to sleep. It is also important to travel and experience different cultures and soak in the beauty of different places on Earth. It reminds us how small we are in the cosmos and what the meaning of our lives truly is. When we travel and relax, we melt away the stress from our careers and our busy schedules and just allow ourselves to be in the moment. We laugh. We sleep. We eat and swim. We build memories with our families and friends who are with us that will be remembered in the future. Vacations allow us to take time out and decrease the number of distractions and input that bombard us every day. This can free up our creativity. We may think of a new business pursuit or opportunity as we stroll along the sand. We may have time to read or learn something new that may boost our sales. We may start a new program at the pool that helps us learn a new language that can build our customer base in other countries. All these scenarios can happen simply because we have time away from our everyday hustle and can concentrate on what we truly want. This includes money and building wealth. I know that I always experience breakthroughs when I can travel and relax my mind to allow creativity to appear. Creativity creates money.

Why?

"Someone's sitting in the shade today because someone planted a tree a long time ago."-Warren Buffett

Why? This is a self-reflection question that everyone must ask themselves during their wealth creation. Why? Why are you getting up and spending 30% of your day at your job, like it or hate it? Why are you spending all your money? Why aren't you spending all your money and investing it? Why do you believe that you're entitled? Why do you struggle and worry about money? Why don't you think you deserve to have money? Why do you play the victim of money? Why don't you have the life you want? Why don't you seek adventure and variety? Why do you stay in your comfort zone? Why do you have your beliefs about money? Why do you hold onto those false narratives about lack of money? Why aren't you rich? Why aren't you spending your time doing what you want to do instead of slaving over a 9 to 5 job? Why don't you move to that new city you want to live in? Why don't you get a promotion or try that new job that's open? Why don't you talk to your spouse about money? Why don't you work as a team to build your wealth? Why don't you spend more time with your children? Why aren't you saving for retirement? Why aren't you saving for children's college education? Why are you spending your money on stuff that doesn't matter? It's in the *why* that shapes your money habits.

Net Worth

"Your net worth to the world is usually determined by what remains after your bad habits are subtracted from your good ones."
-Benjamin Franklin

Isn't that the truth brother! This entire book is based on the fact that the only way to build wealth and get rich is to adopt the good money habits that I talk about on each page and get rid of the ones that are draining your wallet. Net worth doesn't define you as a human being, many important people throughout history didn't have a huge net worth, true. But today, cash is king. It allows you to buy so many things. It gives you safety and security. It buys convenience. It allows you the time and energy freedom that poverty does not. It's in this freedom that makes all the work and sacrifice worth the effort. Every quarter, track your net worth. How much have you saved in cash? How many assets do you own? How much monthly or quarterly cash flow is building in your bank account? Tracking your net worth is your real-world wealth report card. Every quarter it should be increasing. If it's not, then you don't know what the hell you're doing with your money. If it is, then you're following all the principles and ideas that I've been stressing throughout this book. No, you can't take your net worth with you when you die, but you surely can enjoy it and help those around you when you're alive.

Family Time

"Family isn't an important thing, it's everything."-Michael J. Fox

No one spends time cooking dinner together or having game night around the kitchen table. These timeless activities not only build memories with your children but also show them how much you love them. You want to spend time with them. You want to have fun with them. You want to teach them life lessons. You want to make sure they're okay mentally and emotionally. Spending evening and weekend family time together does exactly that. Strong families teach children how to be strong adults. Playing games, watching movies, or doing chores or renovations help to give your children a sense of purpose and belonging to the family that other activities can't provide.

It doesn't cost a lot of money to spend time with your children. Turn off your phones and the computer screens and just spend time doing fun things with your children. When you're doing all the right things with your money, you're less stressed and worried about taking time away from your job or your clients. When you have your money working for you, you now can prioritize the most important thing in your life- your family. So, make sure that you're doing the right things with your money to be able to build these memories with your family and show the love and support that they need to thrive.

Hobbies

"Hobbies are great distractions from the worries and troubles that plague daily living."-Bill Malone

Hobbies are fun. They are an intentional way that you can spend your money. They are also a way to make connections with others that are as passionate about them as you are. Multi- millions of dollars have been negotiated over a round of golf. Pickleball is the new golf where many people get together to play and do business on the side. Wes Moss, author of the book, *What the Happiest Retirees Know*, studied retirees and found that the happiest ones had at least 3 hobbies that they enjoyed throughout their life as well as into their retirement phase. Hobbies help to build community. They get you moving and exercising your body. Like a vacation, they require creativity. Like work, they require focus, perseverance, and time. Having fun and disengaging from reality helps to decrease stress and tension that creeps in. Hobbies are another great way to build strong relationships and network with other people. They always cost money, so make sure you set aside money to spend intentionally on your hobbies and fill your mind and spirit with the joy that they bring. Like vacations, hobbies are little spots in time that allow you to be free from the chaos of the daily grind and like vacations, this freedom can bring about ideas on how to improve another part of your life, including your money.

Email Detox

"Stop letting people who do so little for you control so much of your mind, feelings, and emotions."
-Will Smith

Email has been an effective and sneaky way for marketing psychology to flood your mind. Buy-one-get-one-free sales have been popular for decades, but they used to occur occasionally as seasons and trends changed. Nowadays, there's a sale for every occasion from season changes to national holidays to one-day- only sales. You probably get at least 10 of these emails a day from big corporations. Email is one of the cheapest ways these companies can spend on getting one of their persuasion FOMO messages in front of your eyes, tempting you to click. And it works. According to Luisa Zhou, marketers make $42 for every $1 spent on email marketing. That's a 4200% return on their investment! That's why your inbox is flooded daily with promotions because email is still the king of marketing methods. An easy way to save money and stop impulsive spending is to unsubscribe to their sales. Or set up another email that you give to these companies that you don't necessarily look at daily. This will cut down on your spending impulse and keep your budget on track to build wealth. I have unsubscribed from all companies because I don't want the temptation that I am exposed to daily. If I need something, I check on their website and wait for a sale to occur.

Digital Detox

"Simply put, humans aren't wired to be constantly wired."-Cal Newport

Global Digital Insights reveal that Americans are on social media two and a half hours per day. This accounts for roughly 35% of their daily online activities. And we wonder why we're broke! Many of the online platforms bombard you with marketing messages that control your flow of money which ends up in their pockets and out of yours. There are so many ads and so many influencers pushing products and services in their content. An easy way to avoid all the messaging is to do a digital detox. Eliminate all platforms of social media for 30 days and see what your bank account looks like afterwards. I can guarantee you'll have a surplus in it, especially if you unsubscribe from all the email ads too. I noticed that I was buying a lot of lotions and potions from Instagram, so I just got rid of it. I don't even have the app on my phone. And I never got into TikTok, so that app isn't on my phone either. Getting rid of outside influences has helped me concentrate my energy on getting my money right. I use my phone as an educational device, rather an entertainment device and it has been one of the best changes I've made across the board. I know it can be hard not to know what the latest gadget is or who is doing what, but if you want to build wealth, you need to take control over your money and not allow outside influencers to snag pieces of it along the way. Get rid of it!

Teach Your Kids About Money

"Money grows on the tree of persistence."-Japanese Proverb

How can you teach your child about money and how to build wealth if you don't know about it yourself? This is the very fact that is plaguing our society today. And we must all change this by not only reading the information of this book but implementing it into our lives. We must live with this stuff! By implementing it, we can show our children what it means to build wealth, earn money, and spend it wisely. That's how children learn. They won't necessarily hear you, but they'll see how you act, and they will develop the same behaviors and habits that you have. Do you want your child to be broke and living paycheck to paycheck like you are? Or do you want them to be smart with their money and live within their means? Do you want your child to work until they die, or do you want them to harness the power of compounding and build their wealth over time so they can retire and live their best life? All of us want the best for our children. This must include the best financial education. This must include teaching them where money comes from and how to get it. This must mean learning delayed gratification and saving for a rainy day. This must mean learning how to invest and grow their money so that it can work for them without effort. This is the best gift you can ever give to your child; how to build wealth.

Chapter 8

Whippersnapper Money Habits

This chapter is dedicated to the vibrant energy and unique challenges of financial management in your teens and twenties. In these formative years, developing strong money habits can set the foundation for a lifetime of financial success and security. With the right tools and approaches, young people can navigate their financial journey with confidence and creativity.

Here, we explore the habits that are particularly relevant and impactful for younger generations. These habits address the realities of starting out in today's economic environment—managing student loans, making the most of entry-level salaries, and saving for future goals in a world where traditional financial milestones such as homeownership and retirement seem increasingly challenging.

"Whippersnapper Habits" are not just about managing money—they're about embracing it as a dynamic tool for crafting the lifestyle you want. This chapter provides the insights and tools needed for young adults to take control of their finances early, ensuring they are well-prepared to face whatever financial challenges and opportunities lie ahead. These habits will resonate with you with the spirit and challenges of being young today, empowering you to build a robust financial future from the ground up. Watch the training on the next page.

Invest Early

"Compound interest is the eighth wonder of the world. He who understands it, earns it, he who doesn't, pays it."-Albert Einstein

Theodore Johnson worked for UPS and never made more than $14,000 a year in the 1930s. He thought to himself that he had no money to save, but a friend told him that if he were taxed, the money would be taken out of his account, and he'd never see it. He agreed and started to save 20 percent of his money and it went straight into an investment account. Over more than five decades, that compounded to more than $70 million." According to Brian Preston, founder of *The Money Guy* podcast, $249 invested monthly at the age of 22 years old in a plain old S and P 500 index fund has the potential to grow to over $2 million by the age of 65. Of course, it's difficult when you're first starting your career to save and invest your money, but it's like any muscle. You've got to start training it early so that it will be strong throughout your life. The earlier you start investing, the earlier your money will start earning money and that's a beautiful thing! We don't make money by saving, we make our money through time and compounding growth. The later you start investing, the more money you'll have to save to reach your financial freedom. Isn't freedom worth it?

Establish Credit

"Credit is like a mirror; it reflects your financial reality."
-Unknown

It is good to establish credit when you're young. You can use it to buy a house or for business purposes down the line. What you shouldn't use it for is to buy stupid stuff that you don't need. You shouldn't misuse it or rack it up and not pay it off. Credit can boost your business with inventory if used properly. But building up an emergency fund in cash is better. Credit is like a double-edged sword giving you more freedom to spend than cash does, but you can easily get cut if you misuse it. All you need is one credit card. If you can use it and pay it off monthly and not carry a balance, you can get one that has either money back perks or one that can be redeemed for travel points. I am very cautious to advise you to build too much credit as it's a reflection of your habit of borrowing and paying it back, but credit can be used effectively in many ways. I don't have a personal credit card as I have found myself undisciplined with overspending through the years. I do have a business card that has a low limit that gives me travel rewards that I use to enjoy free flights. But I keep the limit low to not be tempted to overspend. If you find yourself in credit card debt, pay it off, but keep the card open to establish a credit history, but keep the limit very low to help protect you from impulse spending.

Work Harder

"Nothing will work unless you do."
-Maya Angelou

Need cash? Work harder. Want to pay off debt? Work more. Want to build your empire? Work with those that know how to build an empire and mimic their actions. Money is an easy concept to learn, but sometimes is difficult to implement. When you're young, sometimes you may feel entitled to that fancy sports car or that bigger promotion at work, but the older folks will tell you that all of those things take work to obtain. Do more. Be better. Be faster. Have more skills. Try harder. Spend more time. Think out of the box. Master the little things that will really make a difference. If you have a big dream, you'll need a big shovel to get there and the only way to get that big shovel is to work harder. Put in more time. Put in more effort. Be a leader. Take initiative. Be self-motivating and self-reliant. Improve your skills. Improve your pitch. Improve your sales technique. Improve your mindset and beliefs. Improve your methods. Improve your systems. Improve your movements. Improve your plan for getting to your goals. Increase your closing ratio. Increase the amount of time you're spending on a project. Increase the amount of participation you give to it. Listen more. Compromise more. Change more. Work with your team more. Buy more assets. Make more money. Spend more on things that make you happy.

Don't Give Up!

"Believe you can and you're halfway there."-Theodore Roosevelt

Sometimes things don't work out the first time. Sometimes things don't work out right away, they may take more time. You're on your way to discovering your life's purpose and this will take some time for it to develop. Be patient. Be astute. Be diligent and live with intention. Don't worry about what could go wrong, trust that you will be able to make the best out of it in the long run. To rise, you must let go of fear. Never, ever give up. Never surrender to your fears or doubts. Never allow others to control your life, your thoughts, and especially your money. Be in control over all aspects of your life and you will find that you live with adventure and fulfillment. Turn your fears into your greatest strengths. Never be afraid of failing, only fear living a drab and mundane life. Be willing to go through the changes necessary to succeed. Be willing to go the extra mile, to put in extra time, to save exert the extra energy to make your life what you want. It's always worth the extra attention to detail. It's always worth the sacrifice if it's moving you closer to your goals. More effort means more money. More time means more skills. More effort means more results. Never allow your past to dictate your future. That includes your long-held beliefs and thoughts about what you can accomplish in your life. Never ever give up!

Marketing

"The aim of marketing is to know and understand the customer so well that the product or service sells itself."-Peter Drucker

Consumer spending makes up 70% of America's economy. 70%. How do you think all these companies make their money? They use psychological warfare on you to make you feel inadequate and unworthy unless you buy their products and services. It's a dirty way to make people buy, but it's a brilliant way to tap into the human psyche and emotions. If you want to become wealthy, you must learn how to market your products and services. Make people need what you have. Show them that you have what they need to solve their problem. When the problem is great enough, the consumer will part with their money. Sometimes they don't even know they have that problem, but if you paint a picture of the pain it causes, they will want to avoid that pain and buy your product. Pain and pleasure go hand in hand. Lack and abundance. Fear and joy. Self-image and external image. Peer pressure. Fitting in. Ego. Status. Convenience. Jealousy. Regret. Guilt. Envy. Shame. Pride. Anger. If you can learn how to tap into these emotions, you'll be able to draw a line from your customer's wallet to your own. Learn how to market and you'll never be broke again.

Get Rid of Fear

"How we handle our fears will determine where we go with the rest of our lives."-Judy Blum

Fear can hold you back. It can prevent you from getting out of your comfort zone and taking a risk on a new opportunity. That opportunity could be the one that defines your life and your fortune. Never allow fear to get in your way of your dream. Yes, you will fail. Yes, you will lose money. Yes, things won't always go as planned. But anyone who had accomplished anything remarkable in their life will tell you that they too felt fear, but they did that thing anyway. They met that girl. They asked for a sale. They tried a different way. They did that thing that they feared anyways. That's why they're successful. They felt fear, but they took action to see what happened. They took action to make their dreams come true. And you can do the same thing. You too can make your dreams come true if you merely get out of your own way and take one step towards your dream. That's all you must do, take one step every day towards your wealth creation. Make more money. Save more. Buy more assets that pay you. It's a simple formula that has worked for thousands of years. Why not become a warrior for your own life and do the things that you want to do? Want adventure? Take it? Want love? Go find it? Want money? Go get it! You're only young once, take this opportunity now to go for your dreams.

Fail Fast

"Fail early, fail often, but always fail forward."-John Maxwell

It's important when you're young to not be afraid of failure. Failure is where innovation and ingenuity reside. The only way to progress through life is through trial and error and the will to keep going. It seems the older we get, the larger our comfort zone becomes. In my book, *The Art of Discomfort* I discuss the danger and lifelessness of our comfort zones and how it keeps us from the adventure and uncertainty we need as we live our lives. When you're young, it's important to take risks. It's important to try new things. It's important to learn as much as you can and go out on your own. It takes a lot of energy to invest or flip real estate. It takes a tremendous amount of time and energy to start your own business, I know because I did. This is the perfect time to do this, when you're young and full of piss and vinegar. It's easier to fail when you're single and don't have a family to feed. It's easier to learn a new skill when your study skills are fresh from college. You can sleep on your best friend's floor while you get your business up and running when you're young. It doesn't hurt so much. Now is the time to start building your dream so that one day you'll be living it every single day! Now is the time to start building your nest egg that will define your net worth not only to yourself, but your net worth to the world.

Read

"There is more treasure in books than all the loot on Treasure's Island."-Walt Disney

When you get out of college, the last thing you want to do is to continue reading and learning, but this is *exactly* what you must do to build wealth. Like it or not, you only know the basics. Just enough not to be dangerous. The English poems you had to learn, useless. The quantitative chemistry experiments you aced, useless. The amount of beer you drank and all the weed you smoked, useless. Now that you're starting to work, it's time to focus all your attention on building up different skill sets that will not only further your career path but will also ensure that you get rich. You can read books, articles, or blogs for free online from your library. There's also thousands of audiobooks and YouTube videos and online courses that will help you learn the skills that will quantum leap your bank account. Read about how others built wealth. Read about how to build your own consulting business. Read about sales. Read about marketing online. Read about investing. Read about debt elimination. Read about house hacking. Read about minimalism and frugality. Read about side hustle. Read about dividends. Read about private equity and credit deals. Read about gold and silver. Read about franchising. Read about management skills. Read about leadership. Read as much about life as you can.

Embrace Change

"Change is the only constant in life."-Heraclitus

You will learn in life that nothing ever stays the same. Your friends. Your body. Your energy. Your money. It's a good thing if you can embrace the change and make the most of it. Network with others to make strong connections that can be useful in business. Learn new skill sets that can help you get a promotion. Be willing to try and fail on our path to success and wealth. It's the only way to get there. You must change the person you are today, right now, to be the person you need to be when you're financially free. There's a lot of skill sets and education you must obtain and implement before that happens. Change your education level. Change your environment. Change your peer group. Change your morning routine. Change your beliefs and opinions about money and wealth creation that you grew up with. Those won't serve you in the future. Be on the offensive. Learn how to invest and make more money. Begin early and stay late. Change your eating habits which will give you more energy during the day. Only fill your calendar with tasks that will make you grow, change your mindset, and increase your wealth. Stay broke and use your wealth to build a foundation for you to grow as you age. The more flexible and adaptable to change you are throughout life, the wealthier you will become.

Self-Image

"You cannot lead others until you first lead yourself."-John Maxwell

Leaders aren't born, they're made. They're made from skill, determination, ruthlessness, and experience. To get there, you've got to believe in yourself. Success and wealth come from the resilience to do more. It also comes from going the extra mile, making one more sales call or helping one more customer solve their problem. And this all comes from what you believe you're worth, how you see yourself. If you see yourself as lazy, you'll act lazy and do lazy things (or not do successful things). If you want to build wealth and have a family that thrives, you've got to dig down deeply and have the will and the belief that you can do whatever it takes to make it happen. Whatever it takes. You'll sleep on the floor. You'll stay after work late into the night. You'll come in on a holiday to help someone else. You'll not only build the strength and resilience to weather any storm life will throw at you, but you'll also build the confidence that you can get over any obstacle along the way. That's a huge accomplishment if you want to build wealth and a legacy! If you don't believe you can do it, who will? You're only invincible if you believe you are. You're only successful if you believe you are. You're only wealthy if you believe you are. Having a positive self-image is the starting point to all wealth creation and success. Believe you can do it and it shall be done. Believe.

Student Loans

"I had three jobs in college. The best day of my life was when I paid off my student loans."
-Jessica Seinfeld

Student loans account for more than $1.7 trillion. It's the biggest moneymaker of the federal government taking in more than taxes. I accumulated more than $178,000 worth of student loan debt in the 90s. Along with business debt, it took me 13 years to pay it off. I was 39. Student loans are sometimes the only way for someone to get a higher education, but it puts them at a disadvantage. Nowadays, most high schools offer AP and college courses you can take for free. In every city, there's community colleges that have night programs that are affordable and offer the same degrees as four-year institutions. There are students going to private, overpriced colleges that end up with $40,000 salaries and r college debt of $100,000. That's a big problem. If you want to build wealth, you can't have a drag on your savings. My only advice to you is not to take out any loans! Pay as you go. Go to a community college for two years and then transfer and finish at a four-year institution. Or better yet, work and get your degree online. If you do have loans, pay them off ASAP! If you're a parent, start saving for college for your kids as soon as they are born and let them know that they are on a budget.

Go the Extra Mile

"Be so good they can't ignore you."
-Cal Newport

As you're reading this, I hope you are finally realizing that getting rich is easy, but building lasting wealth isn't so easy. Wealthy people know what it takes to build businesses, to invest their money wisely, and to own assets that pay them. It's not easy. They know that it takes a lot of hard work and perseverance to make it happen. That's what you don't see on the outside. You don't see the grind behind closed doors. It's like the professional athlete who has been practicing the same moves since they were 10 years old and now, they make the game-winning shot, and you want to be like him. To be like him, you've got to put in the reps like him. That takes a lot of time, energy, sweat, and perseverance. In wealth creation, being successful takes a lot of skills. These skills take a lot of time to develop. Everyone has unique talents they were born with and must cultivate and strengthen them if they want to create success and wealth. Go the extra mile, especially when you're young. People will notice that you're giving more than the others. They will notice that you care. They will notice that you're listening. They will notice that you're trying to help. It's in this extra effort that loyal relationships are built, and those relationships not only fire your soul, but they also build your wallet. Put in the extra effort and you will be blessed with wealth that goes beyond financial.

Rent

"Renting is not a waste of money. It's buying patience until you're ready to buy a home."-Dave Ramsey

It is wise to rent while you're young. It also may be a good move when you're older too. You can enjoy property amenities like a gym, security, and a pool on the property. You can avoid costly repairs to the roof, windows, and appliances. You can easily move to a different location if you want. Renting makes a lot of sense for a lot of people. The ultimate way to rent is to house hack and own the property. Then other people are paying for your rent and your housing costs are covered or greatly reduced. When interest rates are high and housing prices are inflated, sometimes the only option is to rent. In most big cities where land is scarce, the only way to live is to rent an apartment or townhome. It's cost effective. It allows convenience to restaurants and public transportation, and it allows you to save on other housing costs that homeowners typically need to have like homeowner's insurance and costly repairs. When you're first starting out, share an apartment with a roommate. This further saves you money and allows you to get out of debt and start saving and investing for your future. Rent while it makes sense for you and your financial situation. There's nothing wrong with it and you're not throwing your money away.

House Hack

"Live for free and get rich? What a great combination!"-Unknown

In 2023, the federal government implemented a new program where people could buy a rental property up to 4 units for only 5% down using an FHA loan. However, it must be owner occupied for one year. This means that you must live in one of the units for a year and then could move onto another property purchase or another apartment. This is what house hacking is. You own the property, live in it, and your tenants pay not only for your housing costs, but also for the entire property.

House hacking is one of the easiest ways to start to build wealth when you are young. It also allows you to save money for more properties while you're living there. Housing is one of your highest expenses along with transportation, food, and clothing. If you can lower or even eliminate your housing costs, you can use that money to travel, increase lifestyle, or save and invest. You can set yourself up for financial freedom with only five four-unit properties in the matter of less than a decade. And then you can hire a management team to handle them for you and you can start a family and spend your days doing whatever it is that you want without a boss or money issues. The properties will pay for your lifestyle, and you can enjoy your life the way you want.

Growing Pains

"It takes courage to endure the sharp pains of self-discovery rather than choose to take the dull pain of unconsciousness that would last the rest of our lives."
-Marianne Williamson

There are hundreds of lessons we must learn to be wealthy. We need to learn how to make money. We need to learn how to spend our money. We also need to learn how to save and invest our money. That's a lot of things to learn! Unfortunately, most of us don't learn all of those lessons and we end up being one of the 78% of Americans that are living paycheck to paycheck. If you've gotten this far in this book, I hope you're not going to be one of them! When you're young, you think you're invincible and the good times will always be here. As someone now in her 50s, I can assure you that you are 100% wrong. You will, at some point in your life, face adversity, stress, and grief. Those are all parts of life. You will fail at something. You will experience a health scare. You will have your heart broken. You will lose money. You will get fired or laid off. You will move. You will have to start over. But through all those growing pains, rest assured that you will be a better person because of the trials and tribulations that you endure. This includes your financial journey. You have the luxury of time on your hands, so don't worry about failures.

Be Different

"Strength lies in differences, not similarities."-Stephen Covey

You must be different if you're going to be rich. You can't listen to your parents if they're not financially free by the time you're done with college. You can't go out on the weekends and blow all your money on White Claws and weed like your friends. Sorry. If you want to build wealth and never have to work again, you must control your money and make it multiply. The only way to do that is to save it and invest it in assets that pay you monthly, quarterly, or yearly. It's the only way! 44% of Americans are in credit card debt. 13% of Americans have student loans. 31% have car loans. When your money is going towards debt, there's usually not a lot left over to save and invest. Be different. Don't spend money that you don't have. Pay in cash. Save at least 40% of your income and stay frugal. According to Brian Preston from *The Money Guy* Podcast, every dollar you invest at the age of 20 will multiply 88 times by the time you're 65. That's the power of compound interest. So, when your friends are buying new cars (with loans) and going on fancy vacations, hold your urges back from doing the same. Be different. Continue being frugal and stay broke. Use the money you're making and start investing in real estate or dividend-paying index funds that will not only appreciate over time but will also start paying you cash flow that you can use to double your efforts in building wealth.

Stop Procrastination

"Never do tomorrow what you can do today. Procrastination is the thief of time."-Charles Dickens

You have 24 hours today. What will you do with it? You will sleep 30% of it, so now you're down to 16 hours. If it's a work day, you're now down to 8. What will you do with the remaining 8? Will you sit on your ass and watch Netflix all night? Will you go out and blow your paycheck on drinks and girls? Or will you seize this time and start building your wealth? Will you write out a budget? Will you automate your bills? Will you learn how to invest? Will you learn a new skill set that can help you start a new business? What are you doing with this precious time that you have? When you're young, you usually don't have a family yet and don't have a lot of responsibilities outside of your own life. Take advantage of it! That means that right now, today, is the only time you must take advantage of and improve your path towards financial independence and wealth. Use it. Stop wasting it on fruitless pursuits like video games and house parties. Use it to learn online marketing and content creation. Use it to learn how to house hack and buy your first rental property. Don't put off starting to invest, because the days may be long right now, but the years will be short. You'll wake up one day and realize that you're now 35 and don't have a pot to piss in. Don't wait.

Chapter 9

Messy Middle Money Habits

Now we come to a part of the book that is tailored for those navigating the intricate and often demanding phase of life in their 30s and 40s. Known colloquially as the 'Messy Middle,' this period is characterized by juggling family responsibilities, career progression, and the quest for financial stability and growth. It's a time when the financial decisions you make carry weightier consequences and the need for effective money management becomes paramount.

In this chapter, we explore the specific challenges and opportunities that arise during these middle years. "Messy Middle Habits" is about finding clarity in chaos. By adopting these practices, you can create a robust financial framework that supports both your family's immediate happiness and your long-term financial well-being. These strategies bring order and purpose to your financial decisions, ensuring that you navigate this bustling period with confidence and foresight. Watch the training below.

Avoid Shortcuts

"When it comes to success, there are no shortcuts."-Bo Bennett

For most people, wealth takes time. It takes effort. It takes a lot of energy to endure the daily grind. It takes discipline to save and invest your money every paycheck. It takes patience as the markets go up and down. I get it. But one thing is for sure: don't take shortcuts to wealth. If you hear about a way to be a millionaire overnight, it's a scam, don't do it. If your broke cousin needs money to start his new business that can't lose, it's a scam, don't invest any money with him. If you hear about a stock that's for sure going to go up, it's a scam, don't do it. When you're young, you have the luxury of time. But now, you're in your 30s or 40s and time is slowly ticking away. That means that every dollar that you invest doesn't have as much time as earlier dollars due to multiply and compound your growth. So, it's vital to not lose money during this time. Don't follow shady investments. Don't start flipping houses because you saw a TikTok video about how much money that guy made by flipping five houses. Guess what? They've been doing it for years and know how to do it properly. You don't and you will lose your money. Invest in things that you are knowledgeable about, even if it's just VTI or VOO (ETFs tracking the total stock market or S & P 500). Those are safe investments that should make up the bulk of your portfolio.

4 Walls

"The most significant work we'll do in our whole life is done within the four walls of our home."
-Stephen Covey

It's important when you're in the messy middle to not allow your lifestyle to become inflated. This is where the 4 Walls Rule comes into play. If you can tame the 4 walls, you can enjoy your Starbucks, or your new boots when appropriate without breaking the budget. This is straight from Dave Ramsey's lessons.

1. Shelter: <25% of budget. This includes your mortgage or rent, insurance, property taxes, and HOA fees. If you stay less than 25% you will have margin to invest and build wealth.
2. Transportation. This includes your gas and insurance. Obviously, you should pay for a used vehicle in cash. If you can't, use *The Money Guy* rules: Put 20% down, finance no more than 3 years, and the total amount should be <8% of your income.
3. Utilities. This includes electric, gas, water, trash, and phone bills.
4. Food. This includes groceries and restaurants.

If you can keep these main expenses low, you guarantee the ability to build wealth.

Negotiate Salary

"Successful negotiation is not about getting to a 'yes'. It's about mastering 'no' and understanding what the path to agreement is."
-Chris Voss

You've got a big problem ahead of you and its name is inflation. As you age, the buying power of your money is slowly being eaten away. Things that cost you $10 today will cost you $30 in a decade. So, what are you supposed to do? You must make more money and start investing it so that money multiplies and can help make up the difference in costs. This means you must negotiate your salary. The wrong way to do this is to go to your boss and ask for more money. He'll look over your performance, which is the same as it always is, and tell you no. The right way to negotiate your salary and get a raise is to start being more valuable to your company. That means you must take on more responsibility. That means you must bring in more clients and more revenue to the company. That means you must be more productive and more efficient with your time and efforts. When you do this, record how many new clients and how much money those clients have been worth to the company and how you contributed to that revenue. Then go to your boss and tell him that you would like a percentage of that new revenue as your raise. He won't deny that evidence.

Confidence

"No one can make you feel inferior without your consent." -Eleanor Roosevelt

You're not young anymore. You've got experience. You tried and failed at so many things. It's time for you to feel confident. Confidence at work. Confident in your investments. Confidence in your skills. Confidence in your decision making. If you're not sure about something, now is the time to gain knowledge from a credible resource and implement that knowledge. Don't second-guess your efforts. If you must pivot, make sure that the new path you're choosing will increase your income and wealth-building ability. Now is no time to take a hit as you have too many responsibilities. Be wary of overnight success as it doesn't exist. Feel confident that the plan you made for your life is the right path to follow. You've done the calculations, you're following the steps needed, now continue following the steps. If you hit an obstacle, take a step back, evaluate the situation, and find out what changes you must make and then have the confidence to make them. Learning new skills and implementing those skills in the marketplace takes courage and a lot of energy. Now is the time to be courageous and ambitious in achieving your dreams. Be confident. Be brave. Get the experience you need to make a difference in your life and your wallet.

Comfort Zone

"Life begins at the end of your comfort zone."
-Neale Donald Walsch

We all get into our routines. We get up at the same time. We eat the same things. We surround ourselves with the same people. We basically spend our years living the same day repeatedly like in that movie, *Groundhog Day.* But to make the most of the time we have here, we must break our routines and our habits and jump out of our comfort zones. Sometimes it's difficult to find motivation when the covers are warm and our routines are easy, but to build wealth and reach financial freedom by the time we're 50, we must jump out of comfort and into the big bad cold world out there. It's time for us to grow. It's time for us to improve. It's time for us to grab the bull by the horns and make something happen. We must use our messy middle as a time for continued growth. These years are still vital to building our financial foundation that we can grow and enjoy when we're older. This is no time to lay off the gas pedal. You must continue being more productive and efficient with your time. You must balance your family and your career trajectory, so efficiency and productivity are even more important to your success. Keep learning. Keep growing. Keep improving. Keep networking. Keep saving and investing. Stay frugal. Stay savvy. Stay on top of your finances and stay on track towards your financial goals.

Distractions

"Work is hard. Distractions are plentiful and time is short."
-Adam Hochschild

It's important to silence the noise. Noise can create problems out of nothing. We all have that inner voice that tells us to avoid this or that. We all have kids that are constantly vying for our attention. We have bills to pay. We have spouses to love. We have bosses to satisfy. We have customers to serve. All of this takes a lot of time and energy to make happen daily. But to pursue your dreams and build your wealth, you must carve out some time away from the distractions to work on yourself. An easy way to do this is to join the 5 AM club. Go to bed early and wake up early to make sure you're rested and mentally sharp. Then get to work. Make sure you have a space in your home where you can lock yourself away and focus on a project that will make you money. This time is only for money-making tasks. It's not used to scroll through the internet. It's not used to catch up on social media. This is the time where you do the things necessary to make more money to secure your future and your family. To get into a flow state takes concentration, a deliberate plan of action, and silence to allow your thoughts to surface. You can't think when you're being pulled in all directions by your family, and the daily grind will certainly pull you away. Set the alarm early tomorrow and work on something that will make you more money.

Focus on Your Own Life

"Discovering who you are today is the first step to being who you will be tomorrow."
-Mustapha Lanre Idreez

Run your own race. Stop comparing yourself and your life to your friends or your neighbors. Guess what? They're broke! Yes, you can have fun in life and enjoy all the nice things that a good life has to offer you. But make sure you can afford it first. Most people borrow their life. They take out loans for stuff, for cars, for vacations, and for education. But you're not like that, especially after reading this book! You're focusing your attention and your money on building wealth and financial freedom. You know that this takes time and discipline to make happen. You also know that you must focus on your own household and not worry about what your broke neighbor is doing as he's roaming around the neighborhood in his brand-new Mercedes. You know he's maxed out to the hilt on his finances. Is that how you really want to live? He will have to work until he dies. To me, I'd rather put my money to work for *me* instead. But this means that you must focus on yourself and your own financial goals which doesn't include luxury stuff bought on credit. If you invest in something that pays for that new Mercedes, that's fine. Then when it's paid for, you'll own the Mercedes, and the investment will continue to pay you. That's how you build wealth. Stay focused.

Build Better Systems

"You don't rise to the levels of your goals. You fall to the level of your systems."-James Clear

Every company has systems. The way they sell, the way they market, the way they run internally. Personally, we must build systems too to accumulate wealth as efficiently and effectively as possible. This means we must eliminate all tasks that don't make us money. That may mean mowing the lawn or cleaning the house. That may mean sleeping in. That may mean hiring a personal assistant. That may mean starting a side hustle and using that money to invest in retirement funds. That may mean that we automate our bills and our investments. Whatever system you're using to build wealth, make sure it's the most efficient and effective way. If your bucket is leaking somewhere, you won't be able to achieve financial freedom as fast. If you're wasting your time doing tasks that don't create a sale, then you need to eliminate it. Systems take time and knowledge to build. Once they are operational, they need to keep up with trends and be tracked for optimization. Your wealth systems are the same. You need to make sure that you're tracking your progress and tweak your investments and increase the rate of return and your investment amounts over the course of your career. If you can do this, build better money making and investing systems, you will reach financial freedom without having to work for your money.

Leadership

"Leadership is an action, not a position."-Donald H McGannon

You must become a leader if you want to become financially free. This means you must learn the skills of good leadership. This means you must be a good communicator. You must be able to communicate your vision, goals, and expectations to others. You must also be a good listener and implement the ideas of your team around you. You must build strong relationships with others and use your network effectively. You must be adaptable and be able to adjust to new conditions in the marketplace and new challenges that may arise. You must be an effective decision-maker who is confident and informed. Good leaders have a clear vision for the future and can inspire others on their teams to embrace that vision and work towards it. Leadership comes with integrity and moral principles that can help you to lead by example. Leading others also means being good at delegation and how to leverage the strengths of their teams. You must be good at problem-solving and able to think out of the box as challenges arise. You must take responsibility for not only your actions but their outcomes and be willing to pivot if the path doesn't get you the results you want. And finally, you must motivate and reward yourself and your team for their accomplishments along the way. These are the skills that must be learned to earn more money in a leadership role.

Intuition

"Intuition is the whisper of the soul."-Jiddu Krishnamurti

Intuition is our gut feeling or our sixth sense. It's the ability for us to know and understand something without our conscious reasoning. We know that we should be budgeting and building an emergency fund. We know that we need to avoid lifestyle creep as our income increases. We know that we need to continue saving and investing in our retirement accounts. We know that we shouldn't be swayed to spend due to peer pressure and comparison envy. Then why are we still doing these things? We've got to trust ourselves more and not take advice from people that don't know what they're talking about. The only way to get rich is to save and invest. You must own assets that pay you cash flow and can support your lifestyle. It's the only true path to wealth that's been invented here on Earth. This doesn't mean that you should invest in your brother-in-law's new company just because he's a relative. You must educate yourself first, logically contemplate your investment decision, and trust your gut feeling on whether this investment is the right one or not. If you do this with all your money decisions, you will feel at ease with the financial path that you've created. Educate yourself first, and then be aware of how you feel about your decision and trust in that feeling that you're making the right decision. That may mean a pivot or a better job, that may mean a tweak in your budget.

Declutter

"Out of clutter, find simplicity."
-Albert Einstein

Minimizing your clutter can maximize your life. If you stop spending your money on things you don't need, you'll have that money that you can use to pay off debt, build up an emergency fund, or invest to build wealth. I went through a declutter phase a few years ago. A great YouTube channel to watch to help you declutter is from Joshua Becker. I decluttered my closets. I decluttered my desk. I decluttered my kitchen and bathroom cabinets. I decluttered my clothes. I decluttered my tools. I even decluttered my morning routine and my calendar. Not only do I own less stuff, but I also have less stuff to take care of. My counters are clear and easy to clean. My shelves only have a couple of knick knacks. I have less maintenance to pay for and because of it, I am saving and investing 67% of my income to achieve financial independence. I have a budget. I don't buy things that I don't need. If something is worn out or broken, I throw it out and replace it. Less stuff equals less upkeep and more money in your wallet. Less stuff also means less anxiety and stress. It's so nice to be able to quickly clean my house and relax in a clean house after a long day of work. I'm not tripping over anything or looking at anything that doesn't have a home. Declutter your house, sell what you don't want, and use that money towards your future. Joshua Becker can help!

Smell the Roses

"Today, enjoy those little things about your life, your family, spouse, friends, and job. Forget about the thorns-the pain and problems they cause you and enjoy life."-Bernard Kelvin Clive

We hustle. We work. Our thoughts are going a million miles an hour. We worry about the results. We take care of our careers, our families, and ourselves. But sometimes we forget to slow down and appreciate it all. Sometimes we forget to take some time out of our busy schedules and have some fun. But as we age, we realize that this is all we have- today. Right now, when the kids are screaming and running around, when our spouse is yelling at us, when the deadline is looming on a project, we're ready to launch, right now at this moment, is what defines us. How will we handle the situation? How will we react? Will we even know what's going on around us or are we so caught up in our own thoughts that we don't even notice? When we're so engrossed in our own stuff, that's the time we miss the moment. We miss the blessings in our lives. The people. Our health. Our home. Our stuff. All of it is our true wealth and we need to stop and give thanks that we have all of it, no matter how chaotic it is. Right now, it may seem messy and hectic, but take some time to embrace it and enjoy the little things that make this time wonderful.

Increase Action

"No one is going to make things work out for you. The only way to do so is to utilize every moment of every day at 10x levels."-Grant Cardone

Prioritize and eliminate excuses so you can open doors of opportunities that lie out there. I know that you're busy. You have a young family. You have a house to take care of or you're saving for one. You're saving for retirement. You're saving for college. You're budgeting and making all the right moves with your money. But you have one more thing that you can take advantage of that can make all the difference to your future nest egg and that's energy. You're still young. You still have energy and ambition. You may be tired from home stuff, but you still have dreams and goals you want to pursue. Now is the time to do so. Now is the time to make new connections, to take on new projects at work, to start a new side hustle business. You have energy to pursue the things that could make a huge difference in how much wealth you build over the course of your lifetime. Take advantage of it. You still need to sleep, and you still need to spend time with your family, but you can carve out time during your day to continue to work on your new goals and increase the money supply that's flowing into your life. That's why the 5 AM club is crucial. Get up early and learn new skills, make new connections, and work on things that will make you more money.

Control Ego

"Focus on the past, that's ego. Focus on the future, that's pride. Focus on the present, that's humility."-David Perell

Ego is a funny thing. The older you get; you start to feel confident in your experience and start to rely on past success. But the ego can cloud your judgment and can inhibit your progress if you use it to build the comfort zone around you. You'll find that sometimes things won't work out the first time or how you think they're going to go. That's normal. But ego can enter the situation and mess up the learning process. You must fail before you learn a different way. Controlling your ego in these situations allows you to have faith that things are working out the way they should and that you must figure out what the hurdles are and how to remove them to get to the finish line. Don't allow ego or pride to get in the way of you taking care of your family and creating the wealth that you deserve to enjoy. Constantly learning and growing as a person. Get better. Be humble. Take advice from others that know the solution to your problem and follow it. Make the moves. Develop beliefs. Experience the exposure to success. The older you get, the more you realize that you need to listen more and talk less. You'll learn that the only true success comes from hard work, consistency, and adaptability. Being flexible in any situation is at the core of building wealth.

Balance

"Never get so busy making a living that you forget to make a life." -Dolly Parton

Work life balance is a lie. Like money, there's ebbs and flows and certain periods of time that you will be unbalanced. That's okay. When you're in the messy middle, everyone is tugging at your wallet, your energy, and your time, especially when your kids are very young. Always take some time for yourself to calm your mind, do something fun for yourself, and work on your goals and relationship with your partner. It's easier to create a life with someone else but you've got to be on the same page to make it work. Always carve out some time during your day to work on what you want to work on, especially your money goals. Are you on track to paying off your debt? Are you automating and taking some of the wealth-creation burden off your plate? Are you seeing progress towards your wealth creation? All of this takes time and if you review these questions often, you can relieve the stress that comes with finances while you're building a life and family with your partner. Give them more responsibility. Work as a team. Work on your goals of being a great employee, great investor, and great spouse and parent. When you've checked off all the boxes in life; family and finances, your life will feel so abundant, and your children will feel the love and appreciation that balance can give to them.

Teamwork

"Talent wins games, but teamwork wins championships."-Michael Jordan

You can't be great at everything. That's where your team steps in. If you're a business owner, rely on your team to increase profits and bring your customers more services and more products. It's collective creativity that can move mountains. If you're a corporate employee, bring your unique talents to the team. Be creative. Be a great communicator. Compromise. Be bold and be great at working with others who share your vision and purpose. That's how championships are won. That's how reputations are built. That's how profits are made. And that's how your wealth will be built.

When you can work with a team, you'll be able to innovate and improve any problem in the marketplace. That's where the money is, innovation and imagination. Even if you own your own business, you must be a relentless team player, coaching and practicing your craft with others. It's so important to extrude as much of your own talent as well as that of your team to boost your business's bottom line. When the business wins, you win. Work hard and reap the benefits. When that big promotion comes, take a small piece of it to spend on something fun, and invest the rest into your future. It's in the journey that makes a team strong and unstoppable.

College Fund

"The best investment you can make is in your children."-Unknown

You must be saving and investing in yourself and your future financial freedom before helping your children. The instructions given on a plane before takeoff is to put your air mask on first before helping someone else. This also pertains to saving for your children's college education. There are many ways to save for college. You can prepay using one of your state's prepayment plans. You can open a state 529 or UTMA or UGMA account. These accounts are regulated as to how they grow and how they can be used. A new law was recently passed that allows money in these accounts that aren't used for educational purposes can be transferred to children's Roth IRAs to grow for the future. I am currently saving for my son's education within a separate taxable brokerage account. I found that it best served my needs as I hate federal regulation and have trust issues with rules obligations from the government. My son knows he's on a budget for college and whatever money is left over after his tuition and room/board is paid will then be used to fund my retirement. Saving for your children's college education can save them hundreds of thousands of dollars over the course of their lifetime and can allow them to start saving and investing immediately when they get their first paycheck. This gift is tremendous and can serve as part of your legacy.

HSA

"The best investment you can make is triple tax advantaged."-Unknown

Along with your retirement plans and your college savings, an important account for retirement is to start an HSA or Health Savings Account. The HSA is triple taxed incentivized: you invest with pretax dollars and can deduct your contributions from your income, the money you save grows tax free if you invest it in ETFs, and you can withdraw your money tax free if you use it for a qualified medical expense. It's a triple whammy! You can only contribute to an HSA if you have a high-deductible qualified healthcare plan and there's an annual limit on how much you can contribute. But this is an easy way for you to build up an investment you can use when you're retired. You can use it to pay for your healthcare premiums, copays, prescriptions, dental care, glasses, and medical-related home improvements. If you're 65, you can also use your HSA funds for non-medical purchases, but you will owe tax on those funds. If you're maxing out your retirement plans, are debt-free, saving for college, an HSA plan is another great way to save for future costs. The older we get; we will need more medical care and a fully funded HSA account can help pay for those needs. Make sure to invest that money through your provider so it can grow over time and outpace inflation.

Chapter 10

Middle Age Money Habits

As you venture into your 50s and 60s, the financial landscape begins to shift, focusing sharply on preparing for retirement. This chapter is dedicated to those in their middle age years, a pivotal time when the decisions you make carry significant implications for your financial comfort and security in the later years.

In these crucial decades, the focus is on fine-tuning your financial strategies to ensure a smooth and secure transition into retirement. You'll learn about the essential habits necessary to solidify your financial foundation, manage your investments wisely, and maximize your retirement savings. We'll explore how to assess the readiness of your retirement plans, adjust your investment approach to reduce risk, and increase your financial reserves through strategic saving and spending practices.

This chapter also addresses how to tackle remaining debts effectively, plan for unexpected medical expenses, and consider the timing of Social Security benefits to optimize your retirement income. Additionally, we'll discuss the importance of revising your estate planning to reflect current wishes and circumstances, ensuring that your legacy is managed as you intend. At this age, I aim to equip you with the knowledge and tools needed to navigate these transformative years with confidence as I am going through this time myself personally. By adopting the practices outlined here, you can approach retirement with a robust plan that not only secures your future but also allows you to enjoy your journey towards it. Watch the training below.

Estate Planning

"Plan ahead. It wasn't raining when Noah built the ark."-Richard Cushing

If you don't have a will, create one. If you don't have a living trust, create one. If you don't have a health power of attorney, create one. Throughout this book, you're learning different ways of building wealth. Now it's time to protect this wealth and designate what happens to it when you're no longer alive and using it. Your will names the person who will be responsible (the executor) for distributing your estate. It also designates a guardian for your children if both you and your spouse perish in an accident. You can set up a healthcare initiative inside your will, designating a healthcare power of attorney who will be responsible for your health if you can't make those decisions yourself. If you want to be an organ donor or not be resuscitated in extreme conditions, these decisions can be made through this document, taking those hard decisions off the shoulders of your loved ones. Your living trust is where your assets reside. This is where your money lives. As you accumulate assets, you can title them in your trust's name or hold your trust as the beneficiary if other legal entities such as real estate LLCs are warranted. This helps to shield them from public lawsuits and can avoid probate court ad costs. It's not morbid at all to think about this stuff and you should arrange it as soon as possible.

Cut Ties

"It's okay to cut ties with toxic friends and family that aren't supporting you."-Brenden Dilley

The older we get; the more we lose ties with people that we once were close with. It's a part of life that everyone goes through. But what about those friends and family members that we've hung onto just because we've known them since we were young but they're toxic and negative? It's time to cut ties with them too. You don't have to justify it to anyone. You've got to do what's right for you. You're under no obligation to continue with this relationship. You don't owe anyone anything at this point in your life. Most of the time, it's better to cut as many ties with toxicity and negativity as you can. Who wants to walk on eggshells all the time? It's not fun and you shouldn't have to do it. Embrace people's differences, love them where they're at, but this doesn't mean that you give them your time or your love. Now is the time to fill your life with things you love and enjoy. And that includes people too. Cut ties with those that don't support you. Those that don't make you a better person. Those that you don't have fun with. If you argue with them all the time, cut them out. You'll be so much happier if you're not surrounded by all that stress and chaos. Not everyone is going to love you, that's okay. Cut out those that don't bring you joy and that will give you more time to spend with those that do.

Maximize Contributions

"You may delay, but time will not." -Benjamin Franklin

You're getting older. Time is running out for you to build your wealth. By now, you're over 50, it's time to ramp up contributions to your retirement plans and your taxable brokerage accounts. Anyone that's over 50 years of age can contribute more as a catch-up incentive. So why not? How much are you saving? If you're in debt, eliminate it so you can throw as much at your retirement investments as you can. You're running out of time for compounding to do its magic so the only other way you can build wealth is to throw more money at your investments and get higher returns. Continue paying off debt, including your mortgage so you can use these last remaining years to pad your nest egg. If they're pre-taxed, you'll also enjoy a larger tax deduction for your extra contribution. If you're already maxed out, then start padding a taxable brokerage account. Even though these are after-tax dollars and any returns or dividends that are gained are taxable, who cares? Now is the time to cushion your nest egg so you can make a soft landing into retirement. Now's the time to hustle. You probably don't have a lot of kids around eating away at your income, most people in their 50s and 60s are empty nesters, so now is the time to make as much income as you can and save and invest as much as you can. Build, build, build so that you can achieve financial freedom.

Prepare for Landing

"Retirement is like a long vacation in Vegas. The goal is to enjoy it to the fullest, but not so fully that you run out of money."
-Jonathan Clements

Every day that you're working is a day closer to retirement. Do you know what your financial freedom number is? Do you know what tax implications you'll have when you retire? How will you withdraw from your investments? How will you pay your bills? If you're retiring early, where will you get health insurance and how much will that be? Are you too young to access your retirement plans, and if so, what money have you set aside to pay your bills until you're old enough to access those accounts? Do you have any debt? What do you want to do after you retire? How much will your lifestyle cost? Do you want to travel? How much will that cost? Are you going to downsize your house? Where will you live? Will you continue working part time or do you have enough invested to pay for your lifestyle? What other things are you going to do with your time? How much will those things cost? Any hobbies? Any collections? Any home improvements or projects? Now is the time to look over your retirement plans and make sure that they are adding up to your lifestyle needs. Hire a financial advisor to look over your plans and make sure you're able to hit your numbers *before* you decide to retire.

Set Up Buckets

"There's less stress when the market tanks but your buckets are full." -Unknown

Many financial advisors help you to structure your retirement into bucket accounts. One bucket is for cash and liquid equivalents that you can use in case the market tanks. Most advisors recommend 3 years of cash in bucket one as most recessions in history have lasted around 36 months or less. Of course, if you want more, there's no harm in that. Bucket number two is for more conservative investments, investments like bonds, CD's, high-yield savings accounts, or real estate that have steady, but lower rates of return. Many advisors suggest 4-5 years of money in this bucket so if the market does crash, you can still pull money out of this bucket to fund your lifestyle while still getting a return. The last bucket should be full of the rest of your investments that will give you the biggest bang for your buck. That can include the stock market, index funds, ETF's, private credit and equity, medical debt, and crypto. This bucket will have the most volatility as the economy changes, but in the long run, will help build your wealth and outpace inflation that will eat away your purchasing power. When you're in your 50s and 60s, the main bucket you'll be filling up will be bucket one. You will need a cash account to tide you over in case you retire during a recession time because you don't want to cash out investments when the market is down.

Set Target to Land

"There's a whole new life ahead, full of experiences just waiting to happen. It's called retirement." -Betty Sullivan

Do you know your retirement number? Are you on target to hit it? When? When is your retirement date? What will you do afterwards? Now is the time to start finalizing your plans for retirement. Now is the time to start thinking about when it will be and what that means to your career. Will you give your boss notice? When? Will you sell your business? What does that look like? Who will buy it? How much will you sell it for? What are the tax implications on that sale? Now is the time to start thinking about what that looks like. For the past twenty or thirty years, you've just put your head down and accumulated wealth. You've done all the right things. You've paid off debt. You've grown your skills and income. You've saved. You've invested. You've tracked your progress. You've put your kids through college. Now it's time to settle on a number that's enough for you. Now it's time to settle on a time that's right for you. When is that time? What is that number? Look at your expenses now that you're an empty nester and figure out what your monthly expenses are. Add 15% to that number for home improvements and incidentals and compare that number with your investment number and figure out when you have enough to support yourself and your lifestyle.

Embrace Transformation

"Don't simply retire from something, have something to retire to." -Henry Emerson Fosdick

You're ready to land this plane that you've been working on for most of your life. You've hit your financial freedom number and you're ready to retire. Now what? How are you going to spend all this money that you've worked your entire life accumulating and growing? You can travel. You can help your kids. You can give it away. You can use it to enjoy your favorite hobbies. You can use it to pay the bills. Now is the time to embrace the transition from accumulating and growing your wealth to now spending it on the rest of your life. What does that look like to you? It's an exciting time. I know I can't wait for that date to happen. I plan on traveling and living abroad for 6-8 weeks at a time. I also plan on writing, making more YouTube videos, and coaching people on their money habits. It doesn't matter if I earn a lot of money from these endeavors as I'm doing it to help people, not because of the money. I want to enjoy baking cookies with my grandkids and helping them learn good money habits as they get older. I want to have as much fun in retirement as I can. So, what will you do during your retirement years? Hobbies, travel, grandkids, and charity? Now is a good time to embrace this transformation and plan on how you'll spend your time as well as your money.

Volunteer

"The best way to find yourself is to lose yourself in the service of others."-Mahatma Gandhi

As we get older, we find that our roles in life change. We have experience. We have knowledge. We can see the big picture. We can see how things connect. Our roles change from building and accumulating to that of mentor and teacher. Our services may not be in as much demand anymore, but that doesn't mean our experience is worthless. People may not be banging down our door to hire us, but that doesn't mean we don't add value. At this point in our lives, we don't necessarily need more money. But we have so much to give that it hurts sometimes. That's where mentorship and volunteerism come into play. We can help others that can't afford our expertise. It not only gives them valuable knowledge and insight, but it also gives us a purpose for our time and energy. At some point in our lives, it's not about the money. When that day arrives, we'll realize that fulfillment can be achieved by helping those that need our help. This can be with our time, our effort, or our money. We can build houses. We can visit those in nursing homes. We can run an after-school program. We can teach Sunday School. We can start a YouTube channel. We can tutor. There are so many things we can pass forward to the younger generations that need our help and foresight. Think about how fortunate you are to live here and give back.

Legacy

"Legacy is greater than currency."
-Gary Vynerchuk

Yes, you want to leave your children and grandchildren with wealth. That's why you sacrificed so much of your life for. But how will they continue to build that wealth? Do they know how? That's where other aspects of legacy come into play. Did you pass on the knowledge of frugality, saving, and investing strategies to them? Did you set up investments that keep paying them even after you're gone with instructions on what to do with those investments? Do you instill a sense of confidence, ambition, and knowledge? Did you provide an example of how to lead a fulfilled life, full of love and purpose? Did you give them your time and energy? Do they feel your love? Do they know who you are and what makes you tick? Are they following in your footsteps or are they carving out their own path in life? Are you spending time with your grandkids? Did you set up a college fund for them? Is your estate planning in order? Does your spouse know what accounts you have and where your money is in case you die before he does? Are you helping your kids and grandkids to keep your family traditions alive? Are you teaching them your hobbies? Leaving a legacy is not only about leaving them some money, but also about leaving them with an example of how to live a great life full of family, friends, and adventure. Now is the time to start building that legacy.

Take a Walk

"Breaking up your day by going outside can boost your mood, brainpower, and creativity." -Deborah Grayson Riegel

You haven't seen your spouse in a week because of business meetings or a big project- take a walk together to reconnect. You've got a big deadline and have writer's block and have been staring at a blank screen for half an hour- stop, go outside and take a walk. You've had a stressful day, and the kids are crazy and your head is spinning- go outside and take a walk to clear the chaos. Moving your body and talking with a loved one or smelling the fresh air and looking at the butterflies help to clear our minds of all the things that weigh us down. It helps to lower your blood pressure. It gets your body moving. It helps you reconnect with nature. When we're not actively trying to think of an idea or create a solution to a problem or try to remember something, that's when the idea or solution comes in. When we're forcing ideas, we're creating blocks and resistance for those ideas to come to us. An easy way to clear those blocks and resistances is to do something that doesn't require our logic and reasoning skills. That could be a simple walk around the block. It could also mean taking a break and enjoying a favorite hobby or going to the gym to get your sweat on. If your head is clear, you'll be able to bring more value to your company, thus increasing your income.

Financial Mastermind

"Deliberately seek people who influence you to think and act on building the life you desire."
-Napoleon Hill

Napoleon Hill talks extensively about forming a mastermind in his book, *Think and Grow Rich*. As you near retirement, this can be a valuable group that you're a part of. You can bounce ideas off the people in this group before you make any financial decisions or changes to your plan. You can learn what others are doing in their retirement and alternative areas to invest in that you are unaware of. You can learn different ways of thinking about money and investing. You can see how they're spending their money and enjoying their free time. You can help each other navigate different aspects of retirement. What are some drawdown strategies? How to convert backdoor Roths. What Medicare and supplemental insurance policies you should investigate. When and how to activate Social Security. What tax strategies you should be employing. What AARP deals are out there. How and where to benefit from Senior discounts. Places to travel to. Diet and exercise routines. How to fill your time. Different social groups that you can join. What are some other hobbies to explore? How to create and keep strong relationships with your kids as they age. The benefits of being a part of a mastermind go on and on. If you can't find one, start one.

Medicare

"Medicare provides equal coverage, something that the private sector could not."-Bennie Thompson

Medicare was put into place in 1965 to help hundreds of thousands of older Americans with their healthcare needs. In 2024, it provides healthcare coverage for 18% of Americans or 65 million people. Medicare covers services like x-rays, lab tests, surgeries, doctor visits, wheelchairs, walkers, and most things that are termed '"medically necessary" to treat a disease or condition (Parts A and B). However, there are many facets to health care that Medicare doesn't cover that you should be aware of. There is supplemental insurance that you will have to pay for out of your own pocket which includes two more parts of Medicare including the private Medicare Advantage Pplan (Part C) which goes through private insurance companies and Part D which covers prescriptions. You're first eligible to sign up for Medicare three months before you turn 65. There are many agencies that can help you sign up for any or all the parts that you may need and can help you navigate through the different parts. It is essential to stay as healthy as you can and benefit from all the social programs that have been put into place to help you through your golden years. Take advantage of them. You've worked for them, and the government has taken money out of your paycheck every week to help pay for these systems.

Social Security

"The money that goes into social security is not the government's money, it's your money. You paid for it."-Mitch McConnell

Say what you want about politics and how the federal government handles money, but one benefit that each one of us must take advantage of is social security. You can start taking advantage of a monthly paycheck at 62, 67, or 70. If you delay taking social security after 62 years, your benefits increase 8% every year until you hit your maximum benefit at 70. Every city has a social security office that you must contact and reserve an appointment with to go over your benefits. Make sure if you continue to work part-time that you won't earn more than the amount set by the administration or you will be penalized and taxed on any benefits that you receive. Earned income is frowned upon but income from your investments isn't. Consult with your accountant, financial advisor, and social security to create a plan for receiving your benefits, using your retirement nest egg, and all the tax implications of each. You'll receive your first check the month after you sign up for it. At what age should you sign up? If you've followed my advice throughout this book and have built up a significant nest egg that can support you without social security benefits, then wait until you're 70. If you need before, take it.

Health

"A healthy man wants a thousand things; a sick man only wants one." -Confucius

Two of your main focuses from now on should be fun and your health. If you're smart, you'll combine the two. It's fun to play your favorite sport. Tennis, golf, and pickleball can be enjoyed throughout life. A simple walk with a friend can be fun and get the heart and lungs working. Eat healthy, take your medications, and move your body every day to make sure that you can enjoy all that money that you've worked hard to accumulate over your lifetime. Now is the time to make sure your mind and body are working as efficiently and effectively as possible. Everyone has aches and pains, that's part of our human experience. But that doesn't exclude you from moving. An easy way to help you feel your best is by cutting the carbs and eating more fat and protein. A ketogenic diet has proven to be very effective in warding off heart disease and obesity. I have the best blood work levels when I'm eating less carbs. I feel better and have more energy throughout my day when I'm not eating or drinking simple carbohydrates. Focus on getting the right amount of sleep so that your body has time to remove waste and regenerate your mitochondria for the next day. Keeping yourself healthy means you won't be spending all your hard-earned money on doctors and medical tests. Keep moving and have fun.

Downsize

"Seek not the good in external things but in yourself."-Epictetus

I hate this term, but downsizing is a necessary part of aging. When our kids start their own lives, do we really need a 5000 square foot house with four bedrooms? Probably not. Now is the time to start thinking about making some money from all the upgrades and improvements you've made to your home. Many retirees buy condos or build small ranches free from multiple levels and steps. It's cheaper to take care of, often with no or little maintenance and is easier to keep clean since it has a smaller footprint. Why not choose a new area? Maybe you live in the North where it's cold. Maybe it's time to live somewhere warm and sunny, even in December. Or maybe it's time to ditch America and begin living abroad. There are many retirees on YouTube that started travel channels where they slowly travel to different parts of the world where they want to experience adventure and a cheaper economic system that allows their retirement nest egg to go further. This is the time to start thinking about how you want to live and where you want to live. Do you need the same life that you had while your family is growing up? Probably not. Now's the time to really start thinking about how you want to spend the rest of your days because time keeps marching on whether we want it to or not. Why not take advantage of this time to have fun and explore the world?

Cars

"The car is the closest thing we will ever create to something that is alive."
-Sir Willaim Lyons

Like a new condo or home, it might be time to have a fun car if you're going to stay in America and not live abroad. Why not? You don't have to be a car enthusiast to enjoy going out to a nice dinner with your spouse and rolling up in something nice. The leather seats. The powerful motor. The speakers are playing your favorite music. I grew up with a dad and grandfather that loved cars. They loved racing and working on their own vehicles. I never was interested in doing any of the mechanical work myself, but when I became a dentist, I leased a Silver Mercedes C300. It is only an entry level car, but man, I loved that car. I had a couple more after that and fell in love with its handling and how it made me feel. Unfortunately, my bank account wasn't ready for that vehicle so now I'm driving a 2016 Subaru Outback. I finally got my money right and plan for another Mercedes once I hit my financial freedom number. I plan on buying an asset that pays for my Mercedes so after it's paid off, I will not only own the Mercedes outright, but I will also own the asset that will continue paying me for the rest of my life. If you want a new car, either pay for it in cash or buy an asset that will fund the payment. That's what wealthy people do.

New Connections

"A sweet friendship refreshes the soul."-Proverbs 27:9

As we get older, we'll realize that friends will come and go. If we're lucky enough to live a long time, we'll also realize that most of our friends will die before us. It's important to make new friendships and acquaintances throughout our lifetime, especially as we get older. If you have a large family, you'll find that much of your social circle will revolve around their activities and events. But it's also a must to have outside circles of friends that you can enjoy activities and hobbies with. If you're still working when you're older, it's imperative to continue networking and building your net worth. You may find a group of friends who have similar investment styles as you and you can form a financial mastermind as we've discussed earlier in this book. You may find a group of friends that like to go hiking or golf that will help to keep you active and fit as you get older. You may find a group of musicians that like to go out and party and have fun at clubs and dance the night away. Making new friends and catching up with old ones is an important aspect of our aging process. It's too easy to be isolated from others as our health fails and our memories fade. Stay active. Enjoy your money. Travel. Eat good food. Listen to good music. Laugh and play. Those are the things that will keep your spirit high, your memory sharp, and your body moving.

4% Rule

"The question isn't at what age do I want to retire, it's at what income."-George Foreman

If you've gone the traditional route and saved money in your company's 401k plans, SEPS, Simple Plans, and IRA's, you'll have to determine how much money you will need in retirement and how much you can take out of your plans to fund that number. Many people using this investment strategy form their three buckets- cash, slow growth, and stocks and they pull their money from there. But how much can you pull from your accounts? Of course it depends on what you're invested in. This is a broad statement, but you can pull out 4% as a loose rule. The 4% rule was created from the Trinity study that looked at how long an investment account could last through the ups and downs of the stock market and at what % made it last. They found that 4% was a good mark to use. If you pull out 4%, no matter if the market is going up or down, you will still be building your nest egg enough to sustain your expenses for the rest of your life. Of course, you should consult a financial advisor to make sure you do this correctly, but that's the main rule most retirees follow. I personally don't want to have to sell any of my positions, that's why I've invested in cash flow like real estate, medical debt, oil, dividend index funds, and private equity and credit. These investments pay me monthly and quarterly, so I'm don't have to sell anything.

Drawdown

"Often when you think you're at the end of something, you're at the beginning of something else."
-Fred Rogers

If you have the traditional retirement accounts, there's a certain way to take money out so that you maximize taxes and allow certain accounts to continue to grow tax free.

1. Taxable accounts first. If you're under 59 ½, you can't access your qualified accounts anyways. This may include a cash bridge account that can help you get to 59 ½. This may be other cash or savings. These accounts are the least tax efficient accounts and are subject to capital gains and dividend taxes.
2. Tax deferred accounts are next. These accounts include traditional IRA's, 401 K's, and 403 B's. They are tax deferred and will be taxed as ordinary income when you withdraw from them.
3. The last accounts are your Roth accounts. These accounts are not taxable and can continue to grow as you draw from the other accounts. These accounts can easily be transferred to heirs if you pass before you spend them all.

Of course you should consult with a financial advisor for help.

Chapter 11

Unstoppable Money Habits

As we draw this guide to a close, this chapter is designed to empower you with a curated collection of the most impactful financial habits. These are the practices that, when consistently applied, have the power to transform even the most precarious financial situations into stories of success and stability.

Throughout this book, we have explored a wide range of financial behaviors—from the basic to the complex, from the traditional to the innovative. Now, we distill this knowledge into a potent list of habits that are essential for anyone looking to profoundly change their financial landscape. These habits are not just about managing money; they're about mastering it. They equip you to navigate the complexities of the financial world with confidence and poise.

This chapter does not merely recap what we have learned; rather, it builds on everything that has been discussed, focusing on implementation and consistency. It is about turning theory into action and aspirations into reality. The habits outlined here are universally applicable, whether you are just starting out in your financial journey or looking to refine and optimize your current strategies.

As you read through this chapter, consider each habit not just as a recommendation but as a vital component of a comprehensive financial plan. These are the habits that will not only safeguard your financial future but will also ensure you thrive, regardless of the economic climate.

Let's embark on this final leg of our journey with a clear focus on what truly moves the needle in personal finance. If you implement these unstoppable habits, you'll find that they will define your financial identity and secure your place in a world of ever-changing economic opportunities. Watch the final training below.

Budget Religiously: Master the art of budgeting to know exactly where every dollar is going, ensuring control over your finances. I use Dave Ramsey's "Every Dollar" app. I use the free version and put in my figures to make sure I stay on track every month.

Save First: Prioritize saving by setting aside a portion of your income immediately upon receiving it, even before handling any expenses. You can easily do this through automation. Set up automatic payments for your bills and your investments through HR and your bank app.

Invest Regularly: Start with small, consistent investments to grow your wealth over time, utilizing compound interest to your advantage. When you get a raise, put 75% of it into your retirement investments and keep 25% as a reward. No matter what the market is doing, KEEP BUYING! You want to own as many assets-real estate properties, stocks and bonds, and businesses as you can get your hands on.

Educate Continuously: Commit to lifelong learning about personal finance, investment strategies, and economic changes to make informed decisions. Trends change. Economies go up and down. It's good to take emotion out of your investing and replace it with pure knowledge, reasoning, and later down the road, with experience.

Minimize Debt: Avoid high-interest debt and work diligently to pay down existing debts to free up more of your income for savings and investments. Get rid of student loans, car loans, medical debt, and finally your mortgage. When you don't owe money to other people, you can enjoy life more and you can certainly invest more for your future.

Emergency Fund: Build and maintain an emergency fund covering at least 6 months of living expenses to safeguard against unexpected financial shocks. You will need cash and can store it in a high-yield savings account if you want to earn a little interest on it. But make sure it stays liquid so you can get to it if something bad happens.

Live Below Your Means: Create a lifestyle that spends less than you earn, allowing you to save and invest the surplus. You need a lot of margin in your budget to create financial independence. Minimalism and living simply can help.

Automate Finances: Set up automatic transfers for bills, savings, and investments to ensure timely payments and consistent savings contributions. You can also set up direct deposits into your retirement accounts with HR, so you don't even know your money is working.

Diversify Investments: Spread your investments across different asset classes to reduce risk and maximize potential returns. This includes spreading your investments in things other than the stock market. Real estate, private equity and credit, medical and student loan restructuring, and commodities can provide diversity amongst different sectors to protect your money as economic situations change.

Plan for Retirement: Actively contribute to retirement accounts and plan for your future to ensure financial security in your later years. Earn more money so you can max out your accounts. Once you do, consider HSAs and taxable brokerage accounts that can continue to grow your wealth over time.

Track Your Net Worth: Regularly monitor your net worth to gauge your financial health and progress towards your goals. A quarterly review of your financial statement and net worth can help to keep you on track towards your financial freedom number. You can find free spreadsheets online. I use Robert Kiyosaki's spreadsheet here: https://www.richdad.com/MediaLibrary/RichDad/xsl/Personal_Financial_Statement.xls

Negotiate Better Deals: Hone negotiation skills for salary discussions, service contracts, and large purchases to save money and enhance benefits. Shop sales and buy used when possible. There's nothing wrong with getting the biggest bang for your buck!

Practice Frugality: Embrace frugality where practical, reducing unnecessary expenditures and focusing on value. Spend your money intentionally on only the things that you love. You can buy anything you want, but you can't buy everything all at the same time. Spend money on what's important to you and what makes your life fun and meaningful and forget the rest. Don't be persuaded by manipulative ads or peer pressure. Live your best life and build wealth over time.

Monitor Financial Goals: Regularly review and adjust your financial goals based on life changes, economic conditions, and personal progress. At each stage of life, our goals will change. We go from focusing only on ourselves, to that of our spouse and family. Focus your attention on enjoying your family while simultaneously hitting your financial goals. It won't be easy, but it will be very fulfilling.

Stay Insured: Ensure adequate insurance coverage (health, life, property) to protect against potentially devastating financial losses. Make sure you revisit your policies and premiums every 6 months with an independent insurance agent so they can shop around for a better deal.

Build a Support Network: Engage with financial professionals like advisors, accountants, and knowledgeable friends to gain support and advice. Education is the most important thing when building wealth, besides the actual investing part. Take advice from professionals whose strategies line up with your vision and your end goals.

Focus on Health: Invest in your physical and mental health to prevent high medical costs and maintain your ability to earn an income. There's no use building financial freedom and wealth if you're too sick to enjoy it. Spend money on supplements, a trainer, good food, and your favorite hobby so that you can keep your mind and body strong and disease-free. We all get old, but some of us do it gracefully while others just drop dead. I'd rather be old and enjoy my money as much as possible having fun with the people that I love, doing the things that I enjoy.

Be Adaptable: Stay flexible in your financial strategies to adapt quickly to new financial information or changes in circumstances. Pivot when needed but stay the course. Don't allow a minor financial setback to totally throw you off your financial path. It takes time to build wealth and there will be a lot of obstacles, some you can control and some you can't. Control the ones you can, and recession-proof yourself to weather the ones you can't.

About the Author

Stephanie Aldrich is a general dentist, speaker, trainer, entrepreneur, and author of nine other books and programs, including *The Habit Formula: Life's Success Equation*, *The Habit Formula: A Parent's Success Equation Kid's Edition*, *The Backward Rule: The Ultimate Way to Hit Any Target, The Squirrel Method: How to Find Your Nuts and Get Rich, The 9 Truths: Don't F*ck Up Your Life, Lipstick Philosophy: Daily Wisdom for the Modern Woman, Tiny is Mighty: How Small Changes Create GIANT Results,* and *The Prosperity Paradox: From Financial Stress to Financial Success.*

Coming from humble beginnings in a small town in Ohio, Dr. Aldrich continues to strive for success not only herself but also for others. Knowing that anything is possible drives her creativity to build systems and strategies that anyone can follow to create the life they want to live- and it's easier than you think! If you want to check out her books and programs go to StephanieAldrich.com for more information.

Dr. Aldrich lives in Copley, Ohio, with her loving husband, Steven, and their wonderful son, Noah.

Made in the USA
Monee, IL
04 November 2026

67380064R00105